Puff—

To my favorite chef,
From your favorite gardener
With all my love always

Docky

"Spring '86-88"

HERBS

HERBS

Gardens, Decorations, and Recipes

BY EMELIE TOLLEY AND CHRIS MEAD

TEXT BY EMELIE TOLLEY
PHOTOGRAPHS BY CHRIS MEAD

Design by Justine Strasberg with Betsy Perlman

Clarkson N. Potter, Inc./Publishers
DISTRIBUTED BY CROWN PUBLISHERS/NEW YORK

*To my mother, whose green thumb I
inherited . . . and to my father, whose sense
of design has inspired me.*

C.P.M.

*To my mother, who taught me the joys of
gardening, good food, and above all, the joy
of life. And to Chris, who made it all possible.*

E.T.

Photograph and illustration credits:

Photograph on page 4 of herb garden by Georges Lévêque-France.
Reprinted by permission of Georges Lévêque-France.

Photographs on pages 56, 57, 58, and 59 of the Beverly Jacomini herb garden by
Fran Brennan. Copyright © 1985 by *Houston Home & Garden*. Reprinted by
permission of *Houston Home & Garden Magazine*.

Photograph on page 127 of a basket of roses by Diane Gershuny. Reprinted by
permission of Maria Price and Willow Oak Flower and Herb Farm.

Photograph on page 217 of Château du Domaine St. Martin. Reprinted by
permission of A. Brunet, Château du Domaine St. Martin.

Garden plan illustrations on pages 31, 34, 57, 61, 63, 65, 73, 82, and 87 by Lori
Hoffer. End paper illustration by Beverly Branch.

Recipe credits:

Recipe on page 188 for Pizza con Pancetta from *Cooking with Herbs* by Susan
Belsinger and Carolyn Dille. Copyright © 1984 by Susan Belsinger and Carolyn
Dille. Used by permission of Van Nostrand Reinhold Company, Inc.

Recipe on page 227 of Maria Price's Austrian Peach Cookies with Candied Mint
Leaves, adapted from *Grandma Rose's Book of Sinfully Delicious Cakes,
Cookies, Pies, Cheese Cakes, Cake Rolls, and Pastries* by Rose Naftalin. Copyright
© 1975 by Rose Naftalin. Reprinted by permission of Random House, Inc.

Text copyright © 1985 by Emelie Tolley
Photographs copyright © 1985 by Chris Mead

Published by Clarkson N. Potter, Inc., 225 Park Avenue South, New York, New
York, 10003 and represented in Canada by the Canadian MANDA Group.
CLARKSON N. POTTER, POTTER, and colophon are trademarks of Clarkson N.
Potter, Inc.

Manufactured in Japan

Library of Congress Cataloging-in-Publication Data

Tolley, Emelie.
  Herbs: gardens, decorations, and recipes.

  Includes index.
  1. Herbs.   2. Herb gardening.   3. Cookery (Herbs)
4. Decoration and ornament.   5. Nature craft.
I. Mead, Chris.   II. Title.
SB351.H5T65   1985   635.7   85-9376
ISBN 0-517-55244-2
10 9 8 7

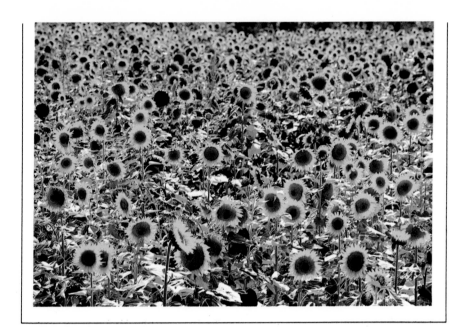

ACKNOWLEDGMENTS

This book took root and grew from the many pleasures and rewards we have found in herbs and our desire to share them with others. The people who have been so generous with their time and knowledge have made it possible, and to all of them we say thank you.

To the following friends, however, we offer our special gratitude:

Charles Cashion, who led us to Nancy Kahan who then took us one step further; and Mary Emmerling and Joe Ruggiero, who guided us through the early stages.

Mary Cronin for the time and effort spent organizing our visits to English gardens; Doreen and Jackie Mead for their long hours of chauffeuring us through the English countryside with unfailing love and good humor, and Fred Mead who uncomplainingly managed on his own; Edward and Margy Dines for their helpful research on English gardens; Elsa and Alan Page for taking us in and making us welcome.

Jacqueline Horscher-Thomas for the many phone calls and unstinting help in France.

Myra Oram, who tested many of the recipes in this book and who was always there with an offer to help; Susan Crispin, Myra Saffery, and Peter Oram, for their unwavering support.

All those people across the United States, and in England and France, who so kindly welcomed us to their gardens, invited us into their homes, and shared with us their ways with herbs.

Betty Desch, who faithfully watered an Englishman's first garden while we traveled.

Betty Lincoln, Richard Sutter, and Donald Wise, who believed in and worked so hard on *Living with Herbs,* the newsletter that was the inspiration for this book, and Judy Rand, who saw its literary possibilities before anyone else.

Pam Satran for her help in turning a phrase.

Tina Strasberg and Betsy Perlman for the sensitive art direction that captured the spirit of *Herbs* so perfectly.

And all those at Clarkson N. Potter, Inc., who gave so much of their time and talent to turn our ideas into a book: Carol Southern; Michael Fragnito and Lynne Arany, who watched over the schedules so attentively; Gael Dillon, who was determined to make this book beautiful; and Robin Feldman, who somehow kept track of everything; and, above all, Nancy Novogrod, our editor, for her encouragement and guidance, her talent for knowing what was needed and what was not, and her constant effort to make *Herbs* the best book possible.

E.T. and C.P.M.

CONTENTS

INTRODUCTION

*H*erbs—*fragrant, flavorful, and colorful—are the most enchanting and useful plants in the garden. The sweetness of valerian, the piney scent of rosemary, the freshness of lavender, are pleasures that lighten and lift the spirit. Pungent thyme, spicy basil, lemony, tart sorrel, give food a special appeal and depth of flavor; silvery artemisias, blue-green rue, deep-green parsley, the shaggy red flowers of bergamot, cheery orange calendulas,*

planted side by side, are a delight for the eyes. Even the sense of touch is affected by herbs—the velvety softness of lamb's ears, prickly stinging nettle, pebbly leaved sage.

This book is a celebration of the capacity herbs have to delight our senses and enhance all aspects of our lives, from our gardens and our homes to our food and our spirits. It is a personal book, filled with ideas for growing

*Spires of mullein, **left**, echo the lines of a wrought-iron gate. At Scotney Castle, in Kent, England, a circular herb garden, **above left**, is contained in a perfect circle of lawn. Garden ornaments can be*

*whimsical, **above right**, like this frog carved by Simon Verity in Hornton stone that hides in a spray of lady's mantle at Barnsley House in Gloucestershire, England.*

1

A rose arbor, **left**, *frames a view of a colonial garden. Railroad tie steps,* **below**, *become part of the garden when creeping thyme is planted between the ties. Yarrow in bloom,* **right**, *adds strong color to the National Cathedral Herb Garden in Washington.*

and using herbs from some of the most talented and innovative gardeners, craftspeople, and cooks in America, England, and France. They approach their gardens and their harvests with a unique point of view that they have shared with us. Their ways with herbs will inspire novice gardeners, as well as those who have been growing, decorating, and cooking with herbs for years.

Both Chris and I started growing herbs because we like to cook and it was convenient having the herbs we wanted to use right there in our gardens. But the more we learned about herbs, the more involved we became. Soon we were growing plants as much for their fragrance and their color as for their taste. We added them to bouquets of country flowers and tucked them into grapevine wreaths—and I even started mixing up potpourris and bath herbs. Our gardens supplied fresh mint to sauce a lamb, silvery artemisia and southernwood to fill out a bouquet, and lavender to sweeten a closet.

Whether you live in a tiny city apartment or on a country estate, you can have an herb garden, too. It could be a simple garden mixing herbs and flowers, a traditional herb garden with

neatly laid out beds, or just a collection of herbs grown in containers. The first part of this book, "Gardening," will show you how: from the light and soil you need, to how to grow herbs from seeds and seedlings, to planning and planting a garden. It includes tips on growing popular herbs and the specifics for planting a window box or a city terrace. It also gives you a look inside some of the world's most innovative herb gardens: a fragrance garden in England planned to give off different scents in the rain and in the hot sun, during the day and during the night; a free-form herbal landscape filled with lavender and rosemary, in the south of France; a lush, informal garden perched at the edge of the sea in Massachusetts; a formally planned mixture of herbs and flowers blooming in the Texas plains.

Once you've grown your herbs, the second part of the book, "Herbal Decorations," will show you old and new ways to use them. You'll find information on when to pick and how to dry herbs for the best results. There are directions on how to mix a fragrant English potpourri that—according to folklore—will inspire thoughts of love; suggestions from experts for

Adelma Simmons, **above far left,** proprietress of Caprilands, strolls through her famous gardens. A rosemary topiary, **below far left,** punctuates the design of a knot garden at Filoli. Assorted herb plants, **below left,** are sold to visitors to the American Museum in Britain. Just a few sprigs of lavender can be turned into a simple heart wreath, **left.** Basil-flavored pesto is as delicious swirled through bread, **below,** as it is on top of pasta.

making herb wreaths; step-by-step instructions for training an ordinary herb plant into an impressive herb standard; special ways to use herbs in Christmas decorations.

The third part, "Herbs in the Kitchen," provides information on how to use fresh herbs and how to preserve your harvest for the winter. You'll discover herbal recipes for everything from pungent sage fritters for nibbling with cocktails to lamb flavored with fresh thyme blossoms and luscious cakes or icy sorbets for dessert. You'll also find kitchen tips and directions for making special dishes from some of the most imaginative cooks and chefs here and in Europe, including Craig Claiborne, Roger Vergé, and Richard Olney.

In our travels for this book, we were constantly discovering new uses for herbs. We saw how their colors, shapes, and textures were combined with flowers to such great effect in lush English borders. Coming from a cold part of the country, we enjoyed learning how rosemary could be part of the landscape on a warm California hillside. We were charmed by the lavender "curtains" we found in Virginia, and dazzled by the herbally seasoned fish *en papillote* we enjoyed on the candlelit terrace of

the Château du Domaine St. Martin and the sublimely simple and beautiful salad that was part of a Provençal lunch with Simca and Richard Olney. In the drawing room of Lady Caroline Somerset's English country house, we saw a bouquet of blue delphinium, gray-green lamb's ears, and yellow-green lady's mantle that has inspired our own herbal flower arrangements ever since—proof that even the simplest use of herbs can open your eyes to new possibilities.

We hope that *Herbs* will help you, too, to discover new ways these unique plants can add beauty to your garden, color and fragrance to your home, and flavor to your foods, and that you'll be inspired to create your own special variations on the ideas you find here. If it does, our travels will indeed have been worthwhile.

GARDENING

*E*ven the smallest herb garden can be a place of enchantment on a warm summer's day. You can watch the bees sip nectar from pale-purple thyme blossoms, inhale the fragrance of mint and lavender, delight in a hummingbird feeding on bright-red bergamot flowers, or admire the diamondlike dewdrop lingering on a leaf of lady's mantle.

These simple pleasures may be enticement enough to start an herb garden, but there are other rewards. Picture yourself dashing to the garden for some fresh fennel to season the fish caught that morning; or picking a bunch of clean-smelling lavender to scent your linens; or gathering an air-freshening herbal bouquet to cheer a sick friend; or creating fragrant dried wreaths and potpourris to revive happy summer memories on cold winter days.

*Two varieties of thyme, **left**, carpet the ground between the border and the central bed in an English garden. More thyme, **above left**, covers the seat of a garden bench. An antique Chinese tub, **above right**, is surrounded by nasturtiums and mint in a Connecticut garden.*

5

For the novice, herbs are the perfect introduction to gardening. Even if you think you have a black thumb—if your past gardens have yielded only bug-eaten tomato plants and wilted flowers—you shouldn't give up gardening altogether before you try growing herbs. They need little special care once the garden bed is prepared, and they resist the diseases and pests that can destroy more temperamental plants. Many herbs grow quickly, rewarding your labors in no time at all with luxuriant foliage in a rich profusion of greens and delicate but colorful flowers.

An antique knife sharpener, **above left,** *is used as a piece of sculpture in an herb garden. Lavender,* **above right,** *borders a brick path.*

Herb gardens are as varied as the personalities and interests of their gardeners. There are traditional gardens and free-flowing landscapes; simplified knot gardens and charming potagers with herbs, vegetables, and flowers. Herbs can be tucked into the border of a flower garden, massed in pots, scattered through rock gardens, or simply planted outside the kitchen door.

Lush plantings, color, and the interesting use of simple geometric shapes all contribute to the appeal of a Massachusetts garden, **left.** *Clustering several of one variety of plant together will have greater impact than growing single specimens, especially when the plants' color and foliage are chosen with care, as with the sharp yellow lady's mantle, pink yarrow, and soft green southernwood,* **above left.** *Roses,* **above right,** *tumble over a white picket fence.*

7

A lacy stand of fennel, roses, and violets, **left,** *is an unusual and attractive way to underplant a tree. At Stillridge Herb Farm in Maryland, wood edgings, wood chip paths, and bricks delineate the plan of a personal version of a traditional garden,* **above.** *Lady's mantle grows at the foot of a gate,* **right,** *which spans an opening in the hedge around this English garden.*

DESIGNING YOUR GARDEN

Before you do anything else, take a realistic look at how much time you're willing to spend on your garden. If you're lukewarm about gardening (although herbs may change your attitude), if you'll resent weeding (even among sweet-smelling herbs), if you'll be bored by picking and pruning the plants (no matter how enjoyable the harvest), or if you've never gardened before, don't undertake a large garden. Settle instead for a little patch of kitchen herbs near the back door, a smattering of plants in an existing garden, a big half-barrel container for a miniature herb garden, or a few clay pots on your windowsill. None of these will overtax your patience, and since most herbs don't require much space, you'll be happily surprised by how many plants you can grow. If you're pleased with the results you achieve in your small garden, you can always plant a larger one the following year.

Where to Put Your Garden

Miniature or grand, an herb garden should always be in a sunny spot. Most herbs do best with at least five or six hours of sun a day. A flat area or a gentle slope facing the sun are ideal locations, but you can also use steep hills or uneven terrain by terracing the land. The few shade-loving herbs like sweet cicely and woodruff can be planted in the shadow of tall plants or in shaded areas of the garden. If you live where cold winds blow, find a place for your garden that will shelter the plants.

And if you're lucky enough to have two or three spots that seem appropriate, choose the one that best suits your purpose: put a culinary garden near the kitchen where you can easily pluck leaves to add to a salad or soup; a fragrance garden near a window or patio where you can enjoy the sweet scents; a decorative garden where you will see it from a window.

Laying Out Your Garden on Paper

After deciding how much time and space you have for a garden, you must then choose the style of garden you want. Will it be an informal grouping of herbs, lush and undisciplined; or a formal garden, its tiny plants placed with geometric precision? You'll see in the gardens that follow that size needn't be a consideration: the smallest garden can be formal, the largest one casual. A border can be either a lush mass of colors and textures or an ordered formal arrangement.

Once you've determined which style you want, lay out your garden on paper. Even the simplest garden will look better if it's planned before planting. Carefully measure the space where you'll plant your garden, then outline it on graph paper,

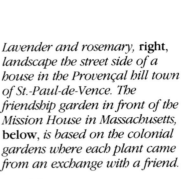

Lavender and rosemary, **right,** *landscape the street side of a house in the Provençal hill town of St.-Paul-de-Vence. The friendship garden in front of the Mission House in Massachusetts,* **below,** *is based on the colonial gardens where each plant came from an exchange with a friend.*

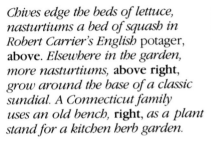

Chives edge the beds of lettuce, nasturtiums a bed of squash in Robert Carrier's English potager, **above.** *Elsewhere in the garden, more nasturtiums,* **above right,** *grow around the base of a classic sundial. A Connecticut family uses an old bench,* **right,** *as a plant stand for a kitchen herb garden.*

allowing one inch for each foot. If the space is more than a tiny patch, divide it further into smaller beds separated by paths. Beds should always be geometrically shaped and symmetrically placed in a formal garden, but can be more randomly arranged in an informal plan. They should be no wider than 4 feet—5 feet if they're accessible from all sides—so you can weed and harvest without stepping in the beds. Paths will also keep your feet dry on wet days and help define the garden's design. And if you plant your garden on a slope or on two or three different levels, you'll need steps.

Now is also the time to decide if you're going to have a fence, wall, or hedge. They can be practical as well as beautiful, protecting tender plants from strong winds, supporting tall plants and vines, and keeping stray animals from running through the garden and trampling the plants.

The last element to consider in your plan is decorative additions such as a sundial or a bee skep, little statues among the herbs, or, if space permits, a bench where you can sit quietly and enjoy your garden's color and fragrance.

What to Plant

After you've planned your garden's physical layout, all that remains is deciding what to plant.

If you intend to cook with the herbs from your garden,

make a list of those you now use most frequently. After you've mapped out space for the essentials, reserve any extra room in your garden for a few herbs you want to learn about: coriander for Mexican, Thai, and Chinese dishes, for example; or cumin for Indian and Middle Eastern food; or borage, sorrel, and burnet for special salads.

If you'll be using your herbs for wreath making and potpourri, choose plants with fragrance and color. You can also base a garden on herbs for tea, medicine, or dyeing, or on collections of the many varieties of a single herb, like thyme.

Planning the Herb Beds

Check the next chapter on individual herbs to find out which of the herbs you've decided to plant are annual, which perennial; how tall each will grow; and how much space each will need in the garden. Then arrange the plants on paper, keeping in mind the following guidelines:

1. When possible, separate perennials and annuals so you won't have to disturb the perennials when you plant or pull out the annuals.

2. Keep tall plants at the back of a border or in the center of an open bed, mid-height plants in the middle, and low-growing plants at the front where they'll create a natural edging. In a formal garden, a low hedge of plants like dwarf lavender,

9

A beautifully turned picket fence, **top,** *surrounds the neat herb garden at the Chatham Shaker Museum. A formally laid out garden,* **above,** *is enclosed with a wall of local Connecticut stone, rather than the more traditional brick.*

hyssop, germander, or santolina often outlines each bed.

3. Space the plants so that each can grow to its fullest. In a very formal garden, separate the plants so that they will all be distinct when full grown. In an informal setting, group them more closely so that they'll seem to blend together.

4. If space permits, cluster several plants of the same kind together for effect.

5. Arrange the plants to contrast their many shades of green, from the silvery green of artemisia to the metallic blue-green of rue. Add interest with the deep reds of opal basil, perilla, and red sage; the yellow leaves of golden marjoram; and the many herbs with variegated green-and-yellow foliage. Try to contrast foliage shapes and textures as well. You can choose from a large variety, such as thin-needled rosemary and lavender, velvety lamb's ears; pleated and scalloped lady's mantle; tiny-leaved thymes, and crinkled horehound and mint.

6. Most herbs flower, and although many have relatively small blossoms, others like bergamot, calendula, nasturtium, and yarrow have rather showy flowers. Be careful how you mix them. A skilled gardener can make a jumble of colors look beautiful, but the inexperienced gardener might do better to keep related colors together: blues, purples, and whites, for instance; or yellows, oranges, and reds.

Once you have completed your plan on paper, it's time to plant your garden.

PLANTING YOUR GARDEN

The first step in planting your garden is to transfer the main outline of your plan to the selected site. After measuring carefully, hammer stakes into the ground at each of the four corners of the plot. If your garden comprises several different sections, put a stake at the corners of each separate piece of the plan. Now outline the shapes by tying string between the stakes. To outline a circle, hammer a stake where the center of the circle should be; then tie a string the length of the radius to the stake. Attach a funnel to the other end. Put some lime in the funnel and swing it in a circle around the stake, moving slowly so enough lime flows through to make a good clear line. The string and lime outlines will guide you as you dig your garden.

Preparing the Soil

At the time you dig the garden, you should prepare the soil, probably the single most important undertaking to ensure the success of your garden. Good soil is a necessity for healthy herbs. They will survive almost anything if they have good drainage and a good friable soil in which to grow. Some soils are so sandy that water passes through before the plants can take advantage of it; others are so full of clay the water doesn't drain off, drowning the roots. You can test the drainage of your soil by watering it well: if the water sits on top instead of draining through, the soil undoubtedly has too much clay; if it is dry to a depth of 1 inch the day after watering, it is probably too sandy.

All gardens should be dug to a depth of at least 12 inches (even up to 24 inches if you're very energetic). Herb grower Thomas De Baggio, who grows and sells exceptionally healthy herbs at his Virginia nursery, Earthworks Herb Gardens, recommends digging a 6-inch layer of compost or sphagnum peat moss into the top 12 inches of the soil, and even suggests adding a little perlite to improve the drainage. "There is almost no soil that doesn't benefit from the addition of humus," he says. "In sandy soils, it helps hold the moisture, while it loosens hard-packed clay soils, letting the water drain away and giving the roots air and room to grow."

Since herbs prefer a neutral or slightly alkaline soil with a pH of 6 to 7½, check the pH of your soil while you're preparing the garden. Simple testing kits are available at garden centers; or you can send a small soil sample to your local Cooperative Extension Service, an arm of the U. S. Department of Agriculture that gives aid to farmers and gardeners. To counteract excess acidity, just dig some lime in along with the humus.

It's also a good idea to dig in a little organic fertilizer when you prepare the beds, to get the plants off to a good start even though, once established, herbs don't need the same amount of fertilizer as other plants in your garden. In fact, while fertilizing will give you lush plants, too much will rob them of some of their fragrance and taste. After the garden matures, just dig a small amount of compost into the soil each fall; and feed the few herbs that require nutrients individually (see listings on pages 14–21 or check with your local nursery to find out which herbs need special feeding).

Buying Your Plants

Once the beds are ready, take out the list of plants you want to grow and note which are annuals, which perennials. Because most perennials are slow getting started, it's better to buy them as small plants from a reliable herb nursery. This also lets you take advantage of the nursery owner's knowledge about the herbs that will grow best in your climate, those that will require special care, and those that are hopeless under local growing conditions. If your nursery doesn't have some of the more unusual herbs you'd like to try, there are herb farms across the country that offer a wide selection of plants through mail-order (you'll find addresses for many of these farms in the directory at the back of this book). Since many herbs need to be divided every year or so, a friend with an herb garden is another good

Herbalist Maria Price, **top,** *picks rue in the Moon Garden she designed for her Maryland farm. Bergamot and other herbs,* **above,** *mix with flowers in the carefully planned but carefree-looking garden of painter Robert Dash's Long Island house.*

11

Sal Gilbertie terraced a hillside, **left,** *for garden space to grow a healthy harvest of herbs and vegetables. Lamb's ears, lavender, and silver mound artemisia,* **right,** *create a lovely palette of greens outside the dining room of a Nantucket restaurant.*

source of plants. Most herb growers are delighted to share the wealth of their garden with others.

Tom De Baggio offers this advice to people who are planning to buy plants.

1. Look for branched plants with strong stems and signs of vigorous new growth.

2. If the plant's color doesn't look right to you, ask about it. Color is often a key sign that something is wrong.

3. If you are like most people and fragrance is one of the important attributes you are seeking in an herb, be sure to pick up the plant (always by the pot) and sniff it. Gently brushing the foliage with your hand helps to release the herb's scent. Never disfigure a plant by pulling off a leaf and tasting it.

4. Make sure the plant is free of insects and disease.

5. The plant should be clearly labeled so you'll know what it is when you get home. If you can't read the label, pick the plant up to see it. Removing the label and then replacing it may injure the plant's tender young roots.

Starting from Seed

Fast-growing annuals can be started from seed, or if you haven't the time or space, buy them from the nursery along with your perennials. If you decide to start from seed, sow them directly in the garden as soon as all danger of frost is past; or start them indoors to get a jump on the season.

Although indoors the seeds may be grown in any container, peat pots that can be set right in the garden without disturbing the young root systems are probably the easiest for inexperienced growers. Use any good potting soil. It's best to work with a predampened mixture: just cut a hole in the top of the bag the soil is packed in and pour in some water. Knead the bag until all the soil is thoroughly damp. Fill the pots to ½ inch below the top with the soil mixture and tamp it down gently. Now plant the seeds according to the directions on the packet.

Set the pots into a waterproof tray so they can be watered from the bottom, then set the tray where the pots will get some light but not sun. Never let the soil in the pots dry out. You can help keep the moisture in by covering the pots with a piece of clear plastic wrap propped up on corner stakes.

Once the seedlings appear, move the pots to a cool, sunny window. It's important they get 5 or 6 hours of sun a day now or they will become leggy. Feed the seedlings with a half-strength

A few herbs are used in quantity in a raised bed garden at Seven Arrows Herb Farm in Massachusetts, **left.**

organic fertilizer every other time you water them. After they have developed two sets of true leaves, pinch them back to encourage the formation of branches. When the little plants are several inches high and look sturdy, and the ground has warmed up with a week or so of good sun, it's time to ready them for their permanent home. Put the plants outdoors in a sheltered spot with filtered sun for a few days, bringing them in at night. This will prevent shock from the change of atmosphere.

Putting In the Plants

Because small plants are easily wilted by the hot midday sun, try to set the herbs out in the early morning, late in the afternoon, or on a slightly cloudy day.

Be careful removing the herbs from their pots. Instead of trying to pull them out, turn the plant upside down, your open hand covering the soil, the stem between your fingers. Gently squeeze the pot; the herb should slide out. If it doesn't, give the side of the pot a few good raps on the ground or a table and try again. If the roots look crowded, gently loosen the outside edges. Then set the plant into a prepared hole, with the top of the roots just below ground level. Scoop a little soil around the roots and water. As soon as the water has drained, fill the rest of the hole, pack the soil down gently around the plant, and water again. Continue watering the plant until signs of new growth are visible, indicating that the roots have established themselves.

Caring for Your Garden

Taking care of the garden once it's planted need not be a chore. "Herbs are easy to care for," says Sal Gilbertie, the largest herb grower on the East Coast and owner of Gilbertie's Herb Gardens in Westport, Connecticut. "You can leave them for two weeks if you have to, and except under the most unusual conditions, they'll survive pretty well. A 10 by 10-foot herb patch will accommodate fifty plants easily," he notes, "and you can care for it in fifteen minutes a week plus another fifteen minutes to harvest the herbs ready to be picked." In that 15 minutes you'll have to do some weeding, particularly in the beginning when vigorous weeds can overcome the young plants; if you have a formal garden, you may need to spend a little more time.

Even though many herbs survive long dry spells in their native habitat, in your garden they need to be watered with some regularity. Mr. Gilbertie suggests you avoid overhead sprinkling "since most herb plants are soft stemmed and susceptible to fungus if they get wet and can't dry off. Giving them enough light and room for air to circulate around them helps, too."

13

*Bush basil, opal basil, parsley,
and marigold make a colorful
display in a kitchen garden
in New England.*

FORTY HERBS TO GROW

Choosing the herbs for your garden is a pleasant task that takes a little time and thought. You'll want culinary herbs if you're a cook; fragrant herbs for potpourris; those that dry well for wreaths and other crafts. You'll need to determine how tall they grow to know where to place them in the bed; whether or not they're annuals or perennials; whether they require sun or shade. This section will give you all the information you need about forty herbs that would be a nice addition to the garden. Decide which ones appeal to you most, but remember: there are hundreds more to explore once you're acquainted with these.

BAY

Laurus nobilis
tender perennial

The pungent leaves of the bay tree are shiny, slightly rippled, and sturdy. They are prized by cooks and wreath makers. Under ideal growing conditions, tiny creamy-yellow blossoms are followed by purplish-black berries, each containing one seed. In temperate climates, plant bay outside in average, well-drained soil, where it's protected from both scorching sun and cold winds. Grow bay in a tub and bring it indoors where winters are frosty. The plant rarely grows over 10 feet tall.

ANGELICA

Angelica archangelica
biennial

Large, round sweetly scented heads of greenish-white flowers top the tall hollow stalks of angelica in early summer. They are followed by a straw-textured fruit containing a brown seed. The slightly bitter leaves resemble celery, but are much bigger. Although the herb is best known for its candied stalks, which are used as decorations for cakes and puddings, its seeds are an important flavoring for liqueurs and gin. Angelica flowers its second year. It can grow as high as 7 feet and the clumps sometimes reach a width of 5 feet. Plant angelica in fairly rich, moist soil in a cool, partially shaded place. Feed it occasionally.

BASIL

Ocimum basilicum
annual

The large, crinkled leaves of lettuce leaf basil and the slightly smaller ones of sweet basil are filled with a warm, spicy fragrance and flavor that is a favorite of cooks. In summer, the leaf stalks are topped with spikes of creamy white flowers. Like other annuals, basil should be pinched as it grows, to increase the yield. Dark opal basil, slightly less pungent, is a colorful addition to the garden with its rich purple leaves. Basil grows approximately 2 feet tall. Give it sun or partial shade, a moderately rich soil, and keep it watered.

BERGAMOT

Monarda didyma
perennial

With its big, shaggy red flowerheads dancing on top of tall stalks, bergamot is one of the handsomest of the flowering herbs. Other varieties have flowers in a range of colors from

15

white through pink and purple to mahogany. Both the long-blooming flowers and the dark-green, slightly toothed leaves have a citrusy flavor and scent reminiscent of Bergamot orange. The leaves are delicious in tea, the flowers are pretty in salads; both are used in potpourris. Favored by hummingbirds and bees, bergamot is also sometimes known as bee balm. It grows from 2 to 3 feet tall. It prefers partial shade and moist, fairly rich, and somewhat acid soil.

BORAGE

Borago officinalis
annual

Borage, with its downy blue-green leaves and delicately drooping clusters of brilliant blue flowers, is lovely if somewhat undisciplined in the summer garden. Although it has no fragrance, the leaves taste slightly of cucumber and can be used in salads and vinegars or brewed into tea. The sugared flowers are pretty decorations for cakes or drinks. Borage grows to heights of 2 to 3 feet on strong stems that, like the leaves, are covered with little hairs. Not fussy about soil as long as the drainage is good, the plants do like lots of sun.

16

CALENDULA
[Pot Marigold]

Calendula officinalis
annual

All summer and into the fall, the bright-orange flowers of the calendula, also known as pot marigold, bloom on sturdy stems among the large, pale-green leaves. The flowers, sometimes single and sometimes double, close at night and occasionally on very dark days as well, then reopen with the morning sun. The dried petals are often used as a substitute for saffron, in soothing skin preparations, and in potpourris. Calendula grows from 1 to 2 feet tall. Plant it in full sun and a rich, loamy soil.

CATNIP

Nepeta cataria
perennial

The heart-shaped, downy, gray-green leaves of catnip, or catmint as it is sometimes called, are topped in mid- to late summer by a mass of purple flower spikes. Cats adore this pretty herb, and many people enjoy catnip tea. It grows from 2 to 3 feet tall and often spreads as far. Another variety (*Nepeta mussinii*), with its blue to purple flowers, is a better

plant to put in the front of the garden because it is shorter, rarely growing more than 15 inches in height. Both are hardy perennials that prefer moist, light, but rich soil. They like some shade but will survive in the sun quite nicely.

CHAMOMILE

Chamaemelum nobile
(Roman Chamomile)
perennial

Chamomilla recutita
(German Chamomile)
annual

Finely divided leaves and daisylike flowers that grow on straight stems above the foliage are common to all chamomiles. German chamomile can be recognized by the hollow, conical yellow center of the flower. It has a sweet scent reminiscent of apples and is the chamomile used for the well-known soothing tea. Roman chamomile has a flower with a flat, solid center. Since the foliage grows no taller than 10 inches, it can provide a soft, lush ground cover. Because it has a slightly bitter taste, it is more likely to be used as a rinse for blond hair than in tea. Another variety, dyer's chamomile (*Anthemis tinctoria*), is a perennial with long-blooming bright-yellow flowers and silvery foliage. It is pretty in bouquets and useful to dyers. Plant chamomile in a slightly acid, fairly rich soil. It likes lots of sun but will tolerate some shade.

CHIVES

Allium schoenoprasum
perennial

The common chive, mild-flavored relative of onions, garlic, and shallots, grows in bright-green clumps of round, hollow leaves that taper to a point. In summer, round, rosy-purple blossoms made up of many individual flowers dot the mounds of green. Both leaves and blossoms are favorites in the kitchen. Chives range in height from 12 to 18 inches. Grow them in rich soil in sun or partial shade. Garlic chives have flat leaves that are wider and grayer, creamy-white flowers, and a mild garlic taste.

COMFREY

Symphytum officinale
perennial

Tall and sturdy, comfrey has large hairy leaves at the base that become smaller closer to the top. The flowers, which change from pink to blue as they open, bloom on graceful sprays during the summer. Comfrey's healing properties are used for minor cuts and skin preparations. The leaves are also a helpful addition to the compost pile. Comfrey grows from 2½ to 3 feet tall. Plant it in moist, fairly rich soil in full sun or partial shade.

CORIANDER

Coriandrum sativum
annual

Pungent coriander grows two sorts of leaves: the lower ones resemble Italian parsley, the upper leaves are delicate and finely cut. The tiny white flowers, tinged with lavender, if left unpicked form a round seed that is warm and sweetly flavored. The fresh herb adds its distinctive taste to the cuisines of China, Mexico, and the Middle East; the seed is ground into curries and baked into breads and cakes. Coriander grows from 1 to 3 feet high and likes lots of sun and a light, well-drained soil.

DILL

Anethum graveolens
annual

Dill lends a graceful note to the

herb patch. The feathery bright-green foliage grows on 3- to 4-foot stems that are topped, when the plant matures, by delicate flat heads of tiny greenish-yellow flowers. Both leaves and seeds are favorite culinary herbs. If you want a continuous supply of foliage, cut the flowers off as soon as they appear. For a harvest of the aromatic small brown seeds, let the flowers mature into seed heads. Plant dill in average, well-drained soil where it will get lots of sun and be protected from strong winds.

FENNEL

Foeniculum vulgare
tender perennial

A tall, graceful plant, fennel has thick, glossy stems covered with feathery green leaves. The 3- to 5-foot-tall stalks are topped with clusters of tiny yellow flowers during the summer which, if left to ripen, turn into aromatic brown seeds. Both leaves and seeds have a strong licorice flavor that is useful in the kitchen. The less stately Florence fennel (*Foeniculum v. dulce*) also has an edible anise-flavored bulb with the texture of celery. Bronze fennel, identical to common fennel except for its coppery color, is a handsome addition to flower borders. Although fennel is perennial in temperate climates, it is generally grown as an annual in the herb garden. Plant it in a sunny spot protected from strong winds.

HORSERADISH

Armoracia rusticana
perennial

Horseradish grows in lush clumps of large, sometimes floppy, glossy green leaves. Some years a single stem of small white flowers grows from the center of the clump. A staple in the kitchen, horseradish is cultivated for the sharp, biting flavor of the root. Plant this hardy 2- to 3-foot herb in loose soil so the root can grow freely. Since it tends to spread uncontrollably, keep it out of the formal garden. Horseradish prefers a cool, moist, but well-drained spot, full sun, and an occasional feeding.

HYSSOP

Hyssopus officinalis
perennial

Bushy hyssop has narrow, pointed dark-green leaves. In the summer they form a handsome background for spikes of blue flowers that are attractive to bees and butterflies. *Hyssopus alba* has white flowers; *Hyssopus rosea,* pink. The slightly bitter leaves and flowers are good in salads or with fatty fish and meats. Hyssop grows from 1½ to 2 feet high and is evergreen in mild climates. It prefers a light, well-drained, alkaline soil and full sun, although it will manage in dappled shade.

LADY'S MANTLE

Alchemilla vulgaris
perennial

Lady's mantle graces herb gardens and flower borders with its mounds of downy scalloped leaves that collect the morning dew. The leaves are neatly pleated before opening to a generous 4 to 8 inches in diameter. The clusters of distinctive yellow-green flowers bloom freely all summer, contrasting handsomely with the blues, grays, and greens in the garden. The flowers are lovely additions to bouquets and the leaves can be used in skin preparations. The mounds can grow as high as 20 inches. Plant lady's mantle in good soil exposed to full sun or in partial shade.

LAMB'S EARS

Stachys byzantina
perennial

The downy gray-green leaves of lamb's ears are covered with soft woolly hairs and can become very large. From early summer, tall, sometimes exotically shaped flower spikes rise out of the leaves, their tips covered with tiny purple blossoms. They are interesting in bouquets, and both leaves and flowers can be dried for wreaths and arrangements. Lamb's ears reaches 1- to 1½-feet in height and tends to spread into any space it can find. Plant it in full sun and well-drained soil.

LAVENDER

Lavandula angustifolia
perennial

The lovely rounded shrubs of lavender add fragrance to the garden from both their spiky leaves and the blossoms that grow above the foliage on long straight stems. Depending on the variety, the flowers can be white, pink, or pale to deep purple and the foliage can range from blue-green to almost gray; the exception is fringed lavender, an indoor plant with deep-green fernlike leaves. Although used primarily for its scent in potpourris, wreaths, and lotions, lavender can also flavor the desserts and vinegars of adventurous cooks. This bushy herb grows from 1 to 3 feet in height. Plant English lavender, the hardiest of the species, if you live in a cold climate. Always put your lavender where it gets full sun and in the dry, rather alkaline sandy soil it prefers.

18

LEMON BALM

Melissa officinalis
perennial

Lemon balm has bright-green heart-shaped leaves filled with a lovely lemony scent and a subtle lemon flavor. The small white flowers that appear in late summer are insignificant and almost hidden by the wrinkled, slightly serrated leaves. The herb's lemony flavor is a nice addition to teas, cakes, and cookies; its scent enhances potpourris. This hardy perennial reaches anywhere from 1½ to 3 feet in height and prefers partial shade but will grow in full sun. Give it rich, moist soil with good drainage and keep it moist during dry spells to prevent yellowing. Another variety, golden lemon balm, is a decorative border plant with pale-gold-and-green leaves. It should be planted in partial shade because too much sun will turn the leaves completely green.

LEMON VERBENA

Lippia citriodora
tender perennial

The graceful branches of lemon

verbena are adorned with light-green pointed leaves and, in late summer and early fall, tipped with delicate spikes of white-to-palest-lilac blossoms. The sweetly lemony flavor is delicious in teas and desserts, the fragrance useful in potpourris. Seldom growing taller than 5 to 10 feet, lemon verbena can be grown in ordinary, well-drained soil in a sunny, sheltered location where the temperature doesn't go below freezing. In the north it must be planted in pots that can be taken indoors for the winter. The leaves may drop when it is moved to a new atmosphere, but after a period of dormancy, new leaves will appear. The plant needs nothing more than ordinary potting soil and an occasional feeding.

MARJORAM

Origanum marjorana
tender perennial

The sweet mild flavor of marjoram comes from the small green oval leaves that grow opposite each other along the length of the stem. The plant is often called knotted marjoram because the small white flowers burst from tiny green knots that form where the leaves join the stem. It is considered by most cooks to be the best of the marjoram family because of its subtle flavor. Hardy only in warm climates, marjoram is generally grown as an annual that rarely gets taller than 12 to 18 inches. Plant it in full sun in a light, rich soil.

MINT

Mentha
perennial

Of all the aromatic mints, spearmint (*Mentha spicata*) and peppermint (*Mentha piperita*) are best known, adding cool, refreshing flavor to candies, gum, ice creams, and other desserts and drinks. The milder, fruity flavored apple mint (*Mentha suaveolens*), with downy gray-green leaves and pineapple mint (*Mentha suaveolens* "Variegata"), whose leaves are bright green with a creamy variegation, are pretty in the garden. So is orange mint (*Mentha citrata*), whose slightly astringent citrus aroma is nice in tea or in skin preparations. Mints are hardy and grow from 1 to 3 feet tall with small flower spikes in shades from white to pink and violet. Plant them in a rich, fairly moist, slightly acid soil in direct sun or partial shade. Keep the fast-spreading roots contained.

MULLEIN

Verbascum thapsus
biennial

Mullein grows to majestic heights.

During its second year, tall stalks ending in spires of small yellow flowers appear out of a rosette of large, woolly, gray-green leaves. It is an attractive addition to the back of the garden or a naturalized setting, and an infusion of the flowers can be used as a rinse to brighten blond hair. Mullein will grow to heights of 6 feet its second year. It thrives in the most ordinary soil providing it is well drained and slightly alkaline, but prefers full sun and a sheltered spot.

NASTURTIUM

Tropaeolum majus
annual

The big, round, bright-green nasturtium leaves are dotted with open-faced flowers in a lovely mix of yellow, orange, red, maroon, mahogany, and creamy white all summer and into the first cool days of fall. Both leaves and flowers have a peppery taste that is good in salads and sandwiches. Mounds of dwarf nasturtiums rarely reach more than 18 inches in height but there's another variety with long stems that creep over the ground, curling around and climbing anything that will support them up to heights of 6 feet. Nasturtiums like full sun, except where it's very hot, and ordinary soil with good drainage.

OREGANO

Origanum vulgare
perennial

Sometimes known as wild marjoram, and a close relative of that plant, oregano has a stronger flavor, and its soft oval leaves that grow in pairs along the stem are larger. In summer and fall the plant is covered with clusters of pretty pink flowers that can be dried for wreaths. Oregano is known for its robust taste and is best used for foods like pizza, where its sharp flavor is not overpowering. Oregano grows from 2 to 2½ feet tall. It prefers full sun and a light, well-drained, somewhat alkaline soil.

PARSLEY

Petroselinum crispum
biennial

The fresh-tasting ruffled leaves of curly parsley grow in graceful clumps about 8 to 12 inches tall. Italian parsley (*P. neopolitanum*) has flat leaves, a somewhat stronger flavor, and grows as high as 20 inches. Undoubtedly the most used culinary herb, parsley enhances the flavor of other herbs as well as foods. Curly parsley is a vitamin-packed garnish and is also a nice addition to an herbal bouquet. Although it's a biennial, parsley is grown as an annual because in the second year the leaves are tough and it flowers and quickly goes to seed. Plant this nutritious herb in rich, well-drained soil in full sun or partial shade. Feed it occasionally.

ROSEMARY

Rosmarinus officinalis
tender perennial

The narrow, spiky leaves of rosemary perfume the air with an unmistakable piney scent. On some varieties the leaves are a shiny dark green with a soft gray underside; on others they are a paler gray-green all over. In the fall, and occasionally in the spring, too, lovely little blue flowers nestle among the sharply pointed leaves. Rosemary's distinctive taste is welcome in the kitchen; its fragrance in potpourris; and the dried sprigs are most useful in wreath making. There is also a less common white-flowered rosemary, *Rosmarinus officinalis alba.* The stems of this bushy plant turn woody with age. Rosemary rarely reaches heights of more than 2 or 3 feet, but in warm climates, under the best conditions, it can grow as high as 6 feet. Rosemary is a perennial evergreen in warm climates, but must be taken in for the winter where temperatures fall below zero. Grow it in sandy, well-drained soil. The aromatic oils will be strongest in full sun, but rosemary will grow satisfactorily in partial shade, too. Another variety, *Rosmarinus officinalis prostratus,* the low-growing prostrate rosemary, has wonderfully twisting branches and is especially suitable for rock gardens and hanging baskets.

RUE

Ruta graveolens
perennial

Rue, bitterest of all the herbs, is also one of the most beautiful. Its pungent blue-green leaves are a unique shape, cut into two or three lobes that seem to balloon out of the leaf. They grow gracefully on woody stems and stay evergreen in warm climates. Several small yellow flowers cluster together at the top of the stems during the summer. If they are not cut, they produce an interesting seed pod that is often used in wreaths and flower arrangements. The dried leaves are a lovely addition to wreaths and winter bouquets, too. Rue grows to 2 feet. Plant it in a slightly alkaline, ordinary, well-drained soil in full sun.

SAGE

Salvia officinalis
perennial

Sage is a bushy plant about 2 feet in height and is evergreen in warm climates. Its strongly aromatic, pebbly leaves are a soft gray-green color. Blooming any time from early to late summer, depending on the weather, the spiky purple flowers add color to the garden and attract bees. Sage is particularly good with fatty meats and fish, cheese, pasta, and rice, and in vinegars. Dried, it is used in wreath making. Grow this relatively hardy herb in well-drained, neutral soil exposed to full sun. There are many varieties besides common garden sage: colorful red sage; green-and-gold variegated sage; tricolor sage (variegated and tinged with red); and the fragrantly fruity pineapple sage with its beautiful red late-summer flowers.

SANTOLINA

Santolina chamaecyparissus
perennial

This aromatic herb with its rough, finely divided silvery-gray leaves

20

looks amazingly like a piece of coral. If left uncut, it will be covered with masses of yellow button flowers on 2-foot stalks during the summer. *Santolina virens* is similar, but the leaves are narrower and dark green, the flowers paler. Fresh sprigs are pretty in bouquets; dried, they are used in wreaths and moth-repellent sachets. Shrubby santolina often spreads as wide as it grows tall and in warm climates will stay evergreen. Plant santolina in an average, slightly acid, well-drained soil in full sun.

SAVORY

Satureja hortensis
(Summer Savory)
annual

Satureja montana
(Winter Savory)
perennial

Both summer and winter savory are peppery, aromatic plants somewhat reminiscent of thyme in both taste and appearance but with bigger leaves. Their pungent flavor is equally useful to cooks. Summer savory is the larger and sweeter plant. Its long narrow leaves grow sparsely along the stem, bronzing slightly in late summer. The small flowers range from white to pink and lavender-blue. Plant summer savory in a rich, light soil where it will get lots of sun and a fair amount of moisture. Winter savory is evergreen in warmer climates. Its

shiny, dark-green leaves are smaller, stiffer, and more pointed than those of the annual; the tiny flowers that bloom along the stem are white or lavender. Winter savory prefers a poorer soil and less moisture.

SCENTED GERANIUMS

Pelargonium species
tender perennial

Scented geraniums with their exotic range of fragrances and differently shaped leaves are among the most pleasant plants to grow. They include the old-fashioned rose geraniums; lemon, lime, and other fruit-scented varieties; spicy scents like ginger and nutmeg; and the more pungent oakleaf varieties. The flowers are insignificant, but the fragrant leaves, whose scent is released by hot sun or touching, are delightful in potpourris and are used to flavor cakes and puddings. Perennial in warm climates, scented geraniums range in height from 2 to 4 feet. In cooler climates, they must be brought indoors for the winter but make excellent houseplants. Give them lots of sun, a well-drained soil, and water during dry spells. Feed potted plants occasionally.

SILVER KING ARTEMISIA

Artemisia ludoviciana v. albula
perennial

Silver king, a plant with graceful stems of whitish leaves, is a decorative addition to the garden, providing a striking background to the brighter greens and flowers of the other plants. The blooms, sprays of little yellowish-white flowers at the ends of the stems, appear in late summer. Dried silver king is a staple for wreath makers, but is lovely, too, in fresh bouquets. A hardy perennial, silver king grows to 3 feet tall. The stems will be taller and straighter in full sun.

TANSY

Tanacetum vulgare
perennial

During the latter part of the summer and into the fall, tansy's clusters of yellow button flowers cap the long stems of feathery bright-green foliage. The leaves have a rather medicinal scent and are used to repel ants, fleas, and flies; the yellow blossoms are dried for wreaths and arrangements. Tansy grows 3 to 4 feet high and will thrive in almost any soil.

TARRAGON

Artemisia dracunculus
perennial

The warm, subtle, aniselike taste of French tarragon is carried in the small pointed leaves that grow the length of its long slender stems. Unlike the disdained Russian tarragon, French tarragon rarely flowers or produces seed so it must be grown from cuttings and root divisions. French tarragon, however, is the flavorful one sought after by cooks. Tarragon will grow from 2 to 3 feet tall and spreads slowly. It prefers sun, but does not thrive in hot, humid climates like that of Florida. Plant tarragon in moderately good, well-drained soil and feed it after harvesting.

THYME

Thymus vulgaris
perennial

The pungent scent of thyme comes from the oil in the small oval leaves of this twiggy little plant. Depending on the variety, the leaves range from dark green to gray-green. Small flower spikes of white, pink, or mauve appear at the end of the stems during the summer and are generally covered with hungry bees. Thyme is a popular culinary herb, but can also be used in potpourris and wreaths. It grows to about 1 foot in height and can be trimmed into a low hedge. Common thyme thrives in full sun and dry, sandy soil, its pungency increasing with the amount of sun.

There are many varieties of thyme, and since their blossoms range from white to magenta and purple, they can make a splendid display in the garden. Lemon thyme (*T. citriodorus*) has a delicate lemon flavor. Creeping thymes like *T. serpyllum, T. coccineus,* and *T. splendens* only grow a few inches high and although not good in the kitchen, make a fragrant ground cover. *T. aureus* and *T. argenteus* are variegated thymes with gold- and silver-tinged leaves respectively.

VALERIAN

Valeriana officinalis
perennial

Valerian's small, pink-tinged, white flower clusters scent the garden during the summer with their strange but not unpleasant fragrance. They grow on single stalks above sprays of toothed and divided leaves, sometimes reaching heights of 5 feet. Although it is pretty in the garden, valerian is generally grown for its root, which has a natural sedative effect. A tea made from the root is a calming bedtime drink. Plant valerian where it is sunny, in soil loose enough to allow the root to develop to its fullest.

VIOLETS

Viola odorata
perennial

The dark-green heart-shaped leaves of violets grow in thick clumps dotted in late spring by fragrant little white or violet flowers, each on its own graceful stalk. Violets' wonderful old-fashioned fragrance has been used to scent linens and colognes for years, but the leaves are also a tasty and nutritious addition to salads and the flowers can be candied to decorate cakes and puddings or picked for bouquets. This hardy perennial never grows to more than 1 foot tall. In temperate climates, violets will do well in full sun or partial shade. In hot areas, it's best to give them protection from the hot afternoon sun. Always plant violets in rich, humusy soil.

WOODRUFF

Asperula odorata
perennial

A beautiful dark-green ground cover, sweet woodruff has whorls of 6 or 8 smooth, shiny, elliptical leaves encircling its stem at approximately 1-inch intervals. In late spring, clusters of tiny white star-shaped flowers appear above the foliage, which never grows more than 12 inches tall. Sweet woodruff has no scent until it is cut and dried, when it gives off the fresh smell of new-mown hay. It is an indispensable ingredient of May wine, and sachets of the dried leaves are popular for scenting linens. Sweet woodruff likes moist, rich, slightly acid soil with lots of leaf mold or compost. One of the few herbs that prefers shade, it soon turns brown if it has too much sun and not enough moisture.

YARROW

Achillea millefolium
perennial

Common yarrow decorates fields and gardens with flat heads of white flowers and finely cut gray-green foliage. Pink yarrow (*A. millefolium v. rosea*), has pink-to-red flowers and bright-green foliage, and fern leaf yarrow (*A. filipendulina*), bright-yellow blooms. Both the white and yellow varieties are lovely in dried bouquets and wreaths. Plant yarrow in full sun, although it can tolerate shade. It will thrive in average soil and can grow up to 4 feet tall.

INFORMAL GARDENS

If you like masses of herbs, green and lush, their delicate or sometimes showy flowers mixing in charming abandon, the edges of one herb blurring into another, plant an informal garden. Like their ancestors—the simple cottage gardens where herbs, flowers, and vegetables grew side by side and the romantic English gardens of the nineteenth century—informal gardens convey an impression of naturalness. They have none of the rigidity of formal gardens with their carefully balanced symmetry and meticulously defined spaces.

However, even these seemingly uncomplicated gardens should have a plan and a sense of structure. Whether it's simply a patch of culinary herbs outside your kitchen door or a more ambitious garden with meandering paths leading from one area to another, an informal garden should never be haphazard. Beds and paths may curve invitingly, beckoning you deeper into a garden with no strict limits; herbs may seem to spill out of the beds, but the garden should still have a feeling of order.

You can define a small space with an old wooden ladder or a wagon wheel, planting each section with one or a variety of herbs; you can enclose a larger space with old railroad ties or local stones, or make a series of terraced beds on the side of a hill. You can mix herbs with vegetables and flowers in a random pattern or use herbs alone. In an informal garden your choice of herbs is unlimited; even those herbs unsuitable for a formal planting because they spread and sprawl onto paths, self-seed, or grow tall will add their simple appeal.

The plants should be placed close together, blending into one another when fully grown. The final effect will be an impressionistic mass of color and texture that may take more thought to get right than a rigidly formal plan.

This Massachusetts garden, an informal mixture of herbs, vegetables, and flowers, was inspired by James Crockett's Victory Garden.

22

A SEASIDE GARDEN

High on a Massachusetts bluff just a few feet from the Atlantic, Pat and Peter Abbott have created a lush garden of fragrant herbs, healthy vegetables, and colorful flowers on land that was once a tangle of cedars and wild grape. The Abbotts painstakingly cleared it, then worked on the soil to turn it into a now fertile field. They gathered seaweed from the shore and spread it out on the rocks for a year to let the rain wash it clean of salt. The following fall the seaweed was worked into the soil and left to decompose and add nutrients over the winter. An abandoned Coast Guard tower nearby provided more free fertilizer—an unlimited supply of pigeon manure.

In planning the garden, the Abbotts consider the height of each plant, when it blooms, and the texture of the foliage. They double crop to increase the yield of the garden, harvesting one crop of early maturing vegetables or annuals and replacing it with another.

Stressing the importance of good soil, Pat Abbott says, "We keep the soil well cultivated all season long with a minimum of effort. Each time we finish working on a row, we pitchfork our way out, so it stays well aerated." It's a good trick to remember. They also keep the soil fertile by mixing in some manure once a year when they rototill the area where the annuals are planted. The Abbotts' biggest problem in caring for the garden is the occasional summer nor'easter, which blows a burning salt spray in from the ocean, turning the plants brown.

Pat talks to her plants and coaxes them along when she transplants them. "Try to transplant on a cloudy day," she advises, "when the heat of the sun won't wilt the plants; and really water well after transplanting."

Wild vines and bushes protect the Abbotts' garden from the strong salt breezes off the Atlantic Ocean just beyond. A scarecrow stands guard over the rows of dill, artemisia, fennel, and flowers that grow in the large (40- by 100-foot) garden.

Pitchforks are kept at the gate, **opposite,** *to remind the Abbotts to cultivate the ground each time they go into the garden. Although the straw farmer scarecrow,* **left,** *has his own cultivator, his only job is to keep the birds from trespassing in the garden.*

27

Valerie Leonard and her daughter, Samantha, water the terrace "herb garden" at their Connecticut home.

A simple and appealing herb garden grows on the patio of Paul and Valerie Leonard's Connecticut home where a few plants poke up randomly among the slates, adapting to whatever small piece of earth they've found. The Leonards delight in the garden's constantly changing face as the herbs reseed themselves in unexpected places or, occasionally, die out and are replaced by another variety. This garden requires minimum care. There's no edging or cultivating of soil and very little weeding to be done, but the scattered plants add fragrance to the terrace and give it a wonderfully casual look.

Sunflowers, **top,** *spring up at random from seeds dropped by birds or carried by the wind. Fragrant creeping thyme,* **left,** *and garlic chives,* **above,** *thrive in the cracks between the stones.*

29

HERBS IN THE WEST COUNTRY

The Victorian stone farmhouse where Lord and Lady Craigmyle spend their weekends is set in the shadow of the monastery that once belonged to the Monks of Bath, close to the old tithe barn, fishpond, and vineyards that are part of the property. Because the house rests on a very steep slope, "bringing machinery in and doing a large garden was almost impossible," says Lady Craigmyle. Instead, the Craigmyles settled on a few small gardens close to the house.

Alan Paterson, a noted English garden designer, was asked to help them with the plans and planting. "We wanted simple

gardens that wouldn't require much upkeep, and since I love using herbs for cooking and as subjects for my paintings, one had to be an herb garden," adds Lady Craigmyle.

Alan placed the herb garden in the walled courtyard between the farmhouse and an old stone dairy, conveniently near the kitchen. The herbs were planted in generous linear sections to form ribbons of contrasting color and texture. Paved paths break up the beds and make the plants easily accessible. There is a strong emphasis on culinary herbs, but the main path running from the farmhouse to the dairy is lined with sweet-scented lavender. The herbs grow abundantly within the walled space, where they are protected from cold winds yet still enjoy many hours of sun each day.

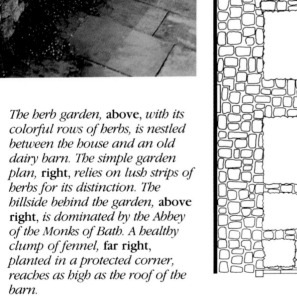

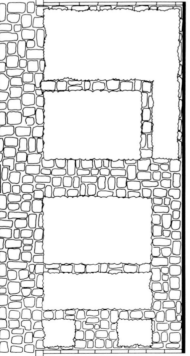

The herb garden, **above,** *with its colorful rows of herbs, is nestled between the house and an old dairy barn. The simple garden plan,* **right,** *relies on lush strips of herbs for its distinction. The hillside behind the garden,* **above right,** *is dominated by the Abbey of the Monks of Bath. A healthy clump of fennel,* **far right,** *planted in a protected corner, reaches as high as the roof of the barn.*

The colorful garden is tucked behind the typical gray-shingled Nantucket house, above right. Basil, parsley, and onions, top, grow side by side with tomatoes just inside the street-side fence. Scented and regular geraniums, center, are massed in an old painted wheelbarrow. French park chairs and a table, above, wait invitingly on the terrace. Everything in the garden, above left, including the day lilies, is edible. The beds are edged with chives, curly parsley, nasturtiums, or even lettuce in the shady areas where it is slower to go to seed. The Kaufmans can enjoy the garden from inside, too, left. More herbs and flowers, opposite, are grown in pots on the steps to the terrace.

A NANTUCKET GARDEN

I don't enjoy reading about gardening. It's like reading about music," says Barbara Kaufman. "You can't. You've just got to experience it." Both Barbara and her husband, Norman, love to garden and have developed their own methods. "I either put lots of one variety of plant in a single spot or I buy a dozen of the same plant and try them everywhere in the garden," she says. "Wherever they do best is where they go the next year. My husband and I like to overplant, too. We don't want to wait for the final effect. I find we never have to pull anything out; nature and the bugs take care of that."

At their house in Nantucket the Kaufmans have created their own enchanted garden. "I think of gardens as belonging to the world of make-believe," says Barbara. "Ours is a fantasy garden rather like in *Beauty and the Beast,* where you go through a tangled hedge to get to the magic garden. Even though it's small, it's self-contained. You enter it through a gate, and once you're inside, you're in a separate world: there's nothing on the outside."

An interior designer, Barbara is also intrigued by the perfect little gardens illustrated in *Peter Rabbit.* "I want my garden to seem like that," she says. "When I plant I think of how it will look rather than what should go where. I even buy herbs from the farm stand because I can't stand to cut those in the garden."

Despite Barbara's yearning for perfection, the herb garden is not off limits to the Kaufman family, including children and pets. The unplanted areas are big enough to accommodate a luncheon table or a spirited game of badminton, "and if the dogs sit in the thyme, we really don't make a fuss," says Barbara.

33

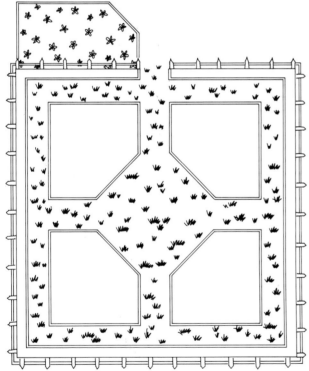

Chris, **top left,** *removed the sod and prepared the soil in the garden before setting in the nursery plants,* **top right.** *Planned to be sympathetic to the small cottage, the garden,* **opposite,** *contains a mixture of herbs, old-fashioned flowers like zinnias and cosmos, and a few vegetables. To separate the garden from the surrounding thicket, Chris put up a plain picket fence. The simple plan,* **above,** *was based on four beds surrounded by a border, edged with pretreated boards.*

AN ENGLISHMAN'S FIRST GARDEN

I've always wanted to have a garden, but thought it would take too much time so I ended up enjoying other people's," says my coauthor Chris Mead. That was before he started photographing herb gardens and talking to the people who grew them. "I suddenly realized," he says, "that herbs don't take as much upkeep as flowers."

With characteristic enthusiasm, Chris immediately began planting a cottage garden at the small summer house he rents on the edge of Shinnecock Bay on Long Island. Inspired by one of the few things he knew about gardening—that preparing the ground was important—Chris devoted himself to improving the soil, digging in peat, fertilizer, and a little lime.

After a rainy spring delayed his gardening efforts, he bought most of his herbs as young plants from the local nursery and only grew a few annuals like nasturtiums and borage from seed. Once the plants were set in place—the vegetables in one section, the herbs concentrated in the three others, and flowers around the border—the only real work was an occasional weeding and weekly watering.

Chris's advice to people who are starting their first garden comes from his own experience: "Be sure and leave enough room for the plants to grow. Don't crowd them together just because the seedlings look so tiny.

"Just after I put in my garden I went away for a few weeks on an assignment. When I got back, I couldn't believe how fast everything had grown, how the small plants were now filling out the bed." Indeed, by midsummer Chris's very first garden had produced a glorious melange of lush green herbs, home-grown vegetables, and brilliantly colored flowers.

A LADDER GARDEN

A ladder garden is a charming way to grow herbs with minimum time spent on planning and building. All you need to do is prepare the soil, then set the ladder in place, and plant. That's what Maureen Ruettgers did on the long narrow strip of land outside the back door of her eighteenth-century Massachusetts farmhouse.

Maureen began growing herbs because she couldn't find many of the varieties she wanted for cooking. Starting with twenty-five snips of culinary herbs she was given by a friend, her gardens have grown to include fragrant herbs for potpourris and those that are useful in wreaths and arrangements. More herbs are grown within a stone wall remaining from the old farm, but most of the herbs come from a large cutting garden, divided into sections, creating a maze where her children like to play. To eliminate weeding, she and her husband mulch the garden heavily with newspaper covered with a thick layer of buckwheat hulls.

She suggests beginning gardeners seek out and talk to as many people who know about herbs as possible and visit their gardens. "I've found people are always happy to give you plants for the garden," she says. She advises starting with culinary herbs in a ladder garden. The clearly defined spaces make it easy to avoid overplanting or a too complicated plan. "Plant each herb in groupings of three," she adds. "Then if one doesn't survive, you won't have to worry."

*The cutting garden, **left**, is divided into simple squares and includes special gardens for each of Maureen's children. In the foreground is the blue-and-yellow herb garden inspired by Monet. A bunny, **above**, painted on stone by one of Maureen's friends, nestles in a bunch of thyme at the edge of the ladder garden.*

Lamb's ears and silvery artemisia, **above left,** *make an effective border in one section of the flower garden. Friends painted the slate markers and made the bee skep,* **above center,** *that add a personal touch to the garden. Maureen's daughter, Polly, grows brightly colored flowers and herbs like pinks, yarrow, and johnny-jump-ups in her garden,* **above right,** *for the potpourris she likes to make. When the yarrow, santolina, and lady's mantle are in bloom,* **below,** *the garden takes on a golden hue. The old drying shed is in the background.*

Each section of the antique orchard ladder, **left**, is planted with a different herb. Maureen Ruettgers, **above**, works on one of the lovely dried arrangements she makes from her harvest. Chive blossoms, **right**, add color to the dried materials.

GLORIOUS INFORMALITY

Glorious disarray is what I like in a garden. No straight lines, no formality. I think the most fulfilling garden is one that's as natural as possible," says Mrs. J. H. Robinson, sitting in the garden at Denmans. Following this philosophy, she has spent the last thirty-odd years in West Sussex, England, creating one of the most delightful English gardens you can imagine. Wide gravel paths meander through the grounds, their edges overlapped by an exuberant array of greenery and flowers that even occasionally poke up through the gravel. "I prefer this rather informal arrangement to borders because you can actually stroll among the plants and enjoy them; and you never get damp feet walking on the gravel paths.

"The plants are constantly seeding themselves everywhere. If the effect is pleasing, I let them be. If not, I pull the seedlings out. It's gardening through elimination rather than planting."

Recently John Brookes, one of England's leading experts on gardens and the author of several books on garden design, has taken over the care of the grounds and established a private landscaping practice and a garden school in the Clock Tower, the old stable block on the property. His approach reflects a certain discipline. "In any kind of a garden you must start from the structure and block out the space," he says. "Then think about the shape of the plant, the form of the foliage—for example, fennel is fluffy, thistles sharp and pointed—and the color."

The walled herb garden at Denmans combines structure and informality. The plan is based on a grid system emphasized by square stones, but the seemingly random placement of the stones and the varying colors, shapes, and heights of the herbs provide a feeling of informality. You could easily adapt this kind of plan to a plot in any size or shape. "But herbs shouldn't be limited to the herb garden," says Mr. Brookes. "Think of them in terms of borders, too." And at Denmans, herbs are mixed with flowers and shrubs all through the gardens.

The herb garden is based on a simple grid system of earth and paved squares. Railroad-tie steps create different levels. John Brookes, **left**, is surrounded by mullein that has randomly reseeded itself in the garden.

Herbs and flowers, **top left**, grow between and over the paving blocks. Various colors of herb foliage and flowers, **left**, make an attractive planting in another part of the garden. Like many of the beckoning paths at Denmans, this one, **top**, is bordered with mullein and lady's mantle that have seeded themselves in the gravel. For convenience, John Brookes grows an assortment of herbs in pots, **above**, just outside the Clock Tower kitchen.

Elsewhere in the garden, **top,** *bronze fennel, rue, catmint, and rosemary make an impressive showing. Calendulas have seeded themselves in the path. Many of the plants are started and then stored in the cold frames in the working part of the garden,* **above.** *Opium poppies,* **top right,** *grow around the pool. Another of the paths,* **far right,** *is edged with variegated sage, mint, and lamb's ears. A terra-cotta pot,* **right,** *contains a collection of thymes.*

Masses of golden lady's mantle, **above,** *sprawl over the edges of the path at the top of the steps that lead from one level of the Simmonses' English country garden to another.*

A COTTAGE GARDEN

Herbs and roses fill the lovely rambling English cottage garden around Eyhorne Manor, an early fifteenth-century house in Kent. When the present owners, Sheila and Derek Simmons, bought the house, which had been added to several times since its early beginnings, what is now an inviting expanse was nothing more than a chicken run and vegetable garden with mounds marking ancient cesspools and two wells. They undertook the task of turning it into the informal garden they wanted, inspired by a vision of its potential.

Although Mrs. Simmons refers to herself as a haphazard gardener, her thoughtfully composed mixtures of color and foliage and the garden's lush but not overgrown look contradict this. To make the garden more interesting, different levels were created around the house. Rambling paths were laid out and stone steps installed to bridge the distance between levels.

"Don't be put off by people who say herbs are dull," Mrs. Simmons says. "Brightly colored plants like golden marjoram and plants with pretty flowers like rose campion, pinks, and lady's mantle add color. And, of course, roses. People sometimes forget that herbs have flowers."

44

The rectangular beds near the house, **left**, easily accessible from the kitchen, are filled with culinary herbs. Marjoram, **top**, creeps over a bench in the garden. In back of the house, an old upright rosemary bush, **center**, evergreen in the mild English climate, reaches the second story window. Younger rosemary bushes, **above**, frame a sheltered garden seat.

45

FREE-FORM HERBAL LANDSCAPES

In the south of France, landscape architect Jean Mus uses fragrant herbs to create free-form landscapes that seem at one with the countryside but have a beauty of color and form that reflects a strong sense of design. Although he has plotted formal gardens on a grand scale, now, he says, "I like to introduce a natural look." Jean uses herbs indigenous to the region, whose climate is similar to California's, where his ideas could easily be adapted.

"It gives me pleasure to make something for another man," he says. "But in order for me to do a good job, there must be a sense of confidence between the owner of the garden and me. I like to have several dinners with him to find out what he likes and doesn't like; how he lives. I visit the site to see what kind of exposure and what kind of soil it has and where the principal wind comes from. Then I go off alone and reflect before I draw up the overall plan." He considers the site's physical limitations first, then his own feelings about the garden and those of his client. "If the views are very different, it's a problem," he says.

Jean finds the quiet colors and interesting shapes of herbs perfectly suited to his natural landscapes. Since most of the herbs he uses have the same soil requirements, they grow well together and pose few problems for the gardener. Their low maintenance is attractive to his clients, many of whom are part-time residents and on vacation when they're in the area.

A free-form sea of lavender dotted with pale-green olive trees, **left and above,** *on the lawn of a château near Cannes is a spectacular example of the way herbs can be used in the landscape.*

47

Jean Mus, **above,** *believes his deep feeling for Provence enables him to design gardens with a special affinity for the region. Unlike conventional borders, those he creates have undulating edges that flow into the landscape and are planted with the same herbs that grow wild on the hillsides. Robust thyme bushes,* **opposite above left,** *delineate a border that curves around a row of ancient olive trees; lavender,* **left,** *fills another border; and thyme, rosemary, and lavender grow in the same bed,* **below.** *Silvery artemisias,* **opposite above right,** *are also used by Monsieur Mus as landscaping plants. Different varieties of rosemary,* **opposite below,** *are selected to border paths or spill over stone walls.*

A NEW ENGLAND LANDSCAPE

Herbs are the basis of the natural-looking landscapes Steven Levine creates in New England. A landscape architect, Steve uses herbs such as thyme, yarrow, mullein, and silver queen artemisia along with edible plants like blueberries and strawberries because they look good, grow fast, and are drought resistant and hardy enough to survive the cold New England winters. The herbs are integrated into the landscape as if they had just grown there, but Steve has carefully worked out the plan to create pleasing blocks of color and texture. Once the original planting is in place, he "let's it go crazy and seed itself as it will."

Creeping thyme and sedum, **above,** *provide carefree landscaping for the entrance to a New England house.*

Pink and yellow yarrow and silvery artemisia are used with other local plants to create a natural-looking, easy-care landscape, **right,** *on the hill behind the house.*

A CALIFORNIA HILLSIDE

For well-known herb authority Norma Jean Lathrop and her husband, Bill, landscaping with herbs was a natural solution to planting the hill in back of their house. The steep terrain needs plants to hold the soil in place, and terracing is a necessity. When Bill Lathrop, a longtime gardener, realized herbs could be used for landscaping, his interest in them was piqued. Because the Lathrops live in southern California where rosemary and lavender are evergreen, they were able to use these plants as the bones of the garden. These herbs line the paths and steps that connect the different levels, releasing their fragrance as people walk by. The terraces, which have been constructed of railroad ties, are planted with a wide variety of herbs that Norma Jean harvests for fragrant potpourris and wreaths, cosmetics and skin creams, and herb teas and other culinary treats.

Rosemary and lavender, both evergreen in California, are used to landscape the steps to the teahouse at the top of the garden.

51

TRADITIONAL GARDENS

I f a sense of order appeals to you, grow your herbs in a traditional herb garden where geometrically shaped beds are laid out symmetrically. These are the neatly planted plots—from simple monastary gardens to elegant French parterres—that are depicted in the pages of medieval manuscripts. Paths separated the beds and gave definition to the plan, and a sundial or fountain often served as a central focal point. The herbs, too, were planted with discipline, each part of a precise pattern and far enough from the next to be seen as a separate form even when full grown.

If you want your garden to be very formal, follow these guidelines. The beds should be crisply edged, the plants kept trimmed and limited to those with neat growing habits. If you are inclined toward a more casual attitude, the basis should still be an orderly plan, but any or all of the other elements can be varied. Substitute local stone for the more traditional brick in walks and walls; use boards for edging instead of a low herb hedge; make the focal point a birdhouse or bee skep instead of a sundial. Plant with abandon, crowding the herbs together within the sections so they blend into a glorious mass as they do in an informal garden, and let them spread and sprawl over the edges, blurring the sharp outline of the plan.

Your traditional garden can be simple or grand, large or small. It can be limited to herbs alone or, for a formal kitchen garden known as a *potager,* include a neat pattern of herbs, flowers, and vegetables. It can be enticingly hidden behind a tall brick wall, set sweetly within a picket fence, or placed in the middle of an open lawn. The plantings can be prim and proper or full of exuberance. But whatever the final choice of style, under it all you'll sense the order you seek.

Johnny-jump-ups, **above right,** *grow in the window boxes of one of the small cottages behind a Nantucket house. Sweet-smelling roses,* **right,** *climb over the roof of the house. A rose-covered arbor,* **opposite,** *frames the view of a Shakespeare garden.*

A TRIBUTE TO SHAKESPEARE

At Fair Gardens, a bed-and-breakfast guest house on Nantucket Island, vacationers enjoy their morning coffee overlooking the fragrant herbs and flowers of a lovely Shakespeare garden. The garden is the result of a happy collaboration between owner Claire Murray, who knew she wanted a garden filled with the herbs and flowers mentioned in Shakespeare's plays, and Betsy Williams, an herbalist from Massachusetts, who helped with the design.

Betsy started by researching and listing all the herbs and flowers that might be planted; then Claire selected the ones she liked best among those that seemed most likely to flourish on the island. Those chosen included a variety of thymes, lavender, rue, parsley, madonna lilies, columbine, and some English daisies that took to the island's climate so well they've seeded themselves everywhere.

The layout of the garden was based on a classic Elizabethan design, with raised beds used instead of care-intensive boxwood edgings because of practical maintenance considerations. Like all gardens, this one changes over the years as plants die out and are replaced, but a periodic refurbishing keeps it at its most beautiful. Betsy, who runs her own herb business creating lovely wreaths and wedding decorations, thinks a formal garden like this needs a lot of research before laying out the final plan and starting to dig.

An informal layout would be easier for first-time herb gardeners. "Keep it simple," she says. "You can appreciate the plants more that way and you won't be overwhelmed by the maintenance. Don't worry too much about the plan. I find an informal garden seems to evolve. I often get plants, then check their cultural needs, and put them where they will do best. Next I look for companion plants that like the same conditions. And suddenly I have a new bed."

*The terra-cotta sundial, **opposite**, is surrounded by thyme. An overview of the garden, **above**, shows how the brick paths define the plan. Surrounded by typical Nantucket houses, **far left**, the garden is hidden from the street by a tall hedge. A foxglove, **left**, is one of the herbal flowers in the English garden near the house.*

55

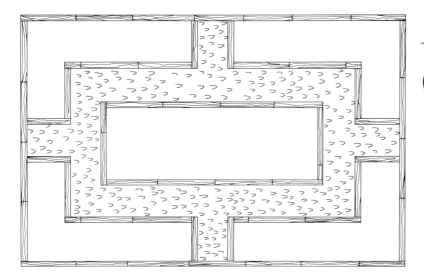

A TEXAS FARM GARDEN

In the Jacominis' garden, **opposite,** *weeds are kept under control in the garden paths with a thick layer of wood chips laid over a sheet of heavy plastic. A folk art rabbit,* **top left,** *marks the center of the garden instead of the more traditional sundial. Pink petunias,* **top right,** *seem even pinker when planted alongside gray santolina. The symmetrical plan,* **above,** *allows plenty of room for herbs, flowers, and vegetables.*

C aring for an herb garden in Texas is no easy matter. The hot Texas sun frequently sends temperatures soaring to 105° during the summer, droughts are commonplace, armadillos dig up the plants, and Texas-sized grasshoppers eat everything.

But interior designer Beverly Jacomini was so determined to have a garden where she could grow herbs, flowers, and vegetables that she took on the challenge at her family's weekend retreat, an old Texas farmhouse halfway between Houston and Austin. Originally the garden was simply a large (36 by 54-foot) rectangle planted in rows. Beverly, a weekend gardener, found the big area overwhelming to care for, so recently, with the help of a local nursery, she divided it into five beds separated by paths and outlined with railroad ties. "Now," she says, "it's much easier to deal with because I can work one area at a time."

Since the nursery concentrates mainly on native Texas plants, they helped Beverly select the herbs, flowers, and vegetables that would grow best in the hot Texas sun. Once mulch and topsoil were added where needed, the plants were set in place. Then a neighbor, Maw Simmons, helped out by

57

watering when Beverly wasn't around, an almost daily necessity in this hot, dry climate.

Now the garden is incredibly lush, a lovely sight from the kitchen window. It provides herbs for seasoning, particularly for the vinegars and pickles Beverly likes to make, and flowers for the house, office, and friends. "Actually, I like to mix herbs and flowers in bouquets, Beverly says. "Two of my favorite combinations are roses with mint and basil with wild flowers. They make the whole house smell fresh."

The well-defined layout of the garden, **opposite,** *contrasts with the open fields beyond. Its color and scent can be enjoyed from the porch,* **top left.** *Flowers and vegetables are planted with herbs,* **top right.** *Beverly's herb-flavored canned vegetables, pickles, and vinegars,* **left,** *are displayed in an antique cupboard. The farmhouse,* **right,** *sits in open fields of wild poppies and Texas bluebonnets.*

59

Weathered wood fences, benches, and random plantings give an informal feeling to the Carters' traditional herb garden.

FAMILY GARDEN IN VIRGINIA

It took Pat Carter a long time to get the garden she'd always wanted. For a mother of nine children, there was not much room for hobbies, and either the family or the garden would have had to suffer. But as soon as the young Carters required less attention, a garden inspired by the formal vegetable gardens at Mount Vernon, George Washington's home on the Potomac, began to take shape on the side of the Carters' late-seventeenth-century Tidewater farmhouse. "I wanted a simplified version that would work with our house," says Pat.

The garden, just outside the kitchen windows, was originally filled with vegetables, but when Pat brought in some chives to edge the tomato bed, herbs began to invade. "I bought one big clump," she remembers. "I didn't know any better, and I separated it into a hundred and fifty little bulbs and planted each one individually around the tomatoes. I got very excited by how quickly they grew and how pretty they were, too, so I went on a rampage and started collecting all different kinds of herbs for the garden." Soon herbs completely replaced the vegetables.

Today the plantings within the geometric beds are rather random. Some of the beds are edged with small boxwood plants, others have weathered fencing around them, and still others are edged with simple weathered boards. The contents of the beds change constantly. "We've found that there are some herbs like sorrel that you can't leave in the same spot because they deplete the soil. And we like to try different things."

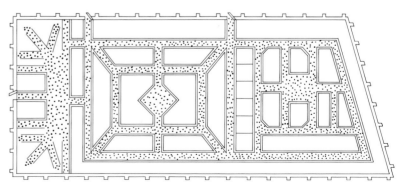

Two beds in the garden are edged with red salvia and devoted to a collection of sages, **left,** *including red-leafed sage, garden sage, variegated sage, pineapple sage, and clary sage. Foxgloves,* **above left,** *add color to the garden in spring. More herbs and vegetables are grown in a small working garden,* **above right,** *by one of the outbuildings, or dependancies, as they are known in Virginia. The plan for the garden,* **below,** *was inspired by a visit to Mount Vernon.*

61

CALIFORNIA HERBING

"You have to be an early riser to garden in California," says Margaret O'Neill. "All the work must be done before eight A.M. when the sun gets hot. When it's hot, it's really hot. And you must love to garden, too, because the climate means you garden all year round, unlike in cooler areas where you have the winter months off. The only rest you get in California is the month of August and the first two weeks in September, when it's so hot the plants give up. Watering is a constant job, too, otherwise the plants wilt."

Margaret's first herb garden was a collection of culinary herbs in pots, but she fast became an enthusiast and decided to put in a proper garden when she and her husband remodeled their house. Now she's become enchanted with fragrant herbs as well and considers this when choosing plants for the garden. "The heat drives away a lot of the fragrance," she says, "so the time I enjoy the plants most is in the early morning or the evening when the dampness in the air brings out their scent."

Another Californian, Tally Ransing, advises friends about to start an herb garden: "Lay your garden out according to where the sprinkler will reach, and dig in lots of compost, twice if possible, before you plant. Then select plants you know you'll use."

Before planting her own garden, Tally did a lot of research. Like Pat Carter's, her final design, though on a smaller scale, was inspired by a trip to Mount Vernon. The sections of the garden were designed with straight sides to accommodate easy-to-install wood edgings. But rather than laying the garden out in simple squares, Tally set the boards at angles to make the paths zigzag so the family's dog couldn't rush pell-mell through the garden harming the plants. Slowed to a harmless pace, the dogs are still able to wander through the garden, picking up the sweet fragrance of the herbs on their coats as they do.

Tally has worked out a system of easy maintenance for her garden. Frequent watering is simply a matter of turning on the automatic sprinkler system that covers the area. "And I have no weeds," she says. "The heavy mulching I learned from my mother, an accomplished gardener, takes care of that. Once a week I do cultivate the soil, though, because it tends to be heavy in spite of the sand we added when we planted." Nourishment for the plants comes from the mushroom compost discarded by a nearby mushroom grower. "The herbs seem to like it better than anything else we've tried," says Tally. When manure is needed, it's obtained from the Santa Anita racetrack, which is at a short distance.

The O'Neills' garden, **opposite top,** *hidden from the street by a curved wall and hedge, has low germander hedges around the beds and thyme growing over the brick walk. The classic sundial,* **above,** *is surrounded by different varieties of thyme. Gray pebble paths delineate the shape of the Ransings' garden,* **opposite bottom,** *which grows in the shadow of an orange tree. Mr. Ransing designed the plan,* **below.**

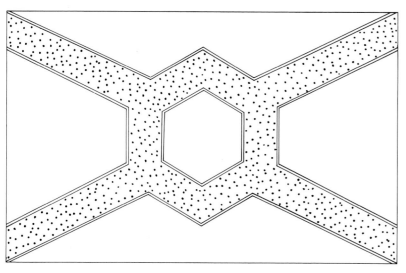

*Herbs, antique roses, and a few flowers, **above**, are mixed informally in the Lewises' herb garden. The drying shed was built to supply additional interest to the garden as well as work space.*

INFORMAL FORMALITY ON LONG ISLAND

Interior designer Robert K. Lewis loves old houses. Even as an eleven-year-old, his room was decorated with a mural of neighboring Alexandria, Virginia, houses he had carefully drawn on pieces of 8½-by-11-inch paper. But he also loves gardening, an interest he shares with his wife, Joy, and when they bought their present Long Island home, their time was split between work on the house and the designing and planting of an herb garden. "I like formal geometric designs informally planted," says Bob Lewis, offering a perfect description of the garden he installed.

The garden's design is organized by straight brick paths punctuated by box balls at two diamond-shaped intersections. The bricks are held in place with a metal band running along the outside edges of the paths. Young boxwood hedges, planted around the beds, will eventually grow to a height of 3 feet to contain the rather casual planting. Even in winter, the boxwood and brick walks are a strong graphic statement, a pleasing sight from the upstairs windows. To supply additional interest, Bob built a small drying shed behind the garden and an arbor along one side. A terrace under the arbor provides a shady spot to sit during the warm summer months.

Bob uses the herbs from his garden—including antique roses, mint, gray-leaved lamb's ears, and golden oregano—in fresh bouquets, which he and Joy present to friends. He also often includes bunches of dried herbs in his design work. "It's surprising how appropriate they seem in even a very elaborate stainless-steel kitchen," he says. The Lewises use their harvest for cooking, too. For one example of their culinary ways with herbs, see page 198.

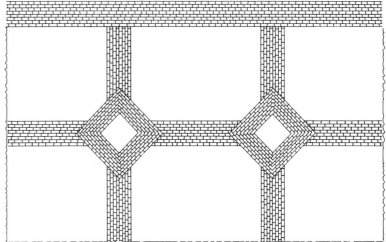

The pattern in the brick paths, **left**, emphasizes the garden's diamond shapes. Nasturtiums, **top**, spill out over the paths. Bob Lewis likes the idea of johnny-jump-ups and alyssum, **right**, growing here and there among the bricks. He starts them, then lets them spread and reseed themselves, eliminating any that seem superfluous. The plan, **above**, for the garden is simple but graphic.

Old painted furniture, **opposite,**
provides storage and work space
in the shed, which also doubles as
a convenient flower room where
Bob arranges the herb and flower
bouquets, **left,** he enjoys creating.
Meadow rue, **top,** blooms in the
garden. A bundle of aromatic
herbs, **above,** hangs on the door
of the shed.

67

GARDENING IN THE COLONIAL STYLE

My house has been evolving since the eighteenth century and I wanted my garden to have the feeling of that time," says Elizabeth Keith. Her Connecticut garden, based on the colonial tradition of mixing herbs, vegetables, and flowers, is very much in keeping with the house.

Mrs. Keith started gardening during World War II. "I had to learn to raise a victory garden," she says. But even with all her years of experience, she called upon garden designer Rudy Favretti to help her work out the planting of this garden. A circle of culinary herbs marks the center of the garden, which is surrounded by inner quadrants filled with vegetables and outer quadrants planted with perennial and annual flowers. Fruit trees grow just outside the fence. A personal touch is added by the dovecote and the arbor seat covered with grapevines at one end of the garden.

Mrs. Keith dries some of the herbs and flowers for arrangements traditional enough to suit the house. Much of the produce is preserved in the freezer or turned into jams and jellies. "The garden gives me a great deal of pleasure," she says, "and it fills all my needs for herbs, fruits, and flowers."

A beautifully shaped wooden gate, **above**, *spans the opening in the stone wall. Standard rose trees mark the four corners of Mrs. Keith's colonial garden,* **right**, *and a circle of herbs surrounds the central dovecote.*

The shape of the fence pickets and posts, **top**, are as carefully thought out as the garden itself. Each shingle of the custom-made dovecote, **above**, was hand-carved. Stone steps, **right**, lead from the garden to the house. One of the two rose-covered arbors, **far right**, provides a quiet spot in which to read or simply to sit and enjoy the garden.

70

AN HERB WALK

Sandy Greig learned about herbs from her first landlady, who grew fennel, parsley, and oregano for her kitchen. After discovering the difference these herbs made in cooking, Sandy wanted to learn more and ended up running her own herb farm in Red Hook, New York, a few hours north of New York City.

Sandy's fourteen small theme gardens are arranged along an herbal walk, open to anyone who wants to wander through and enjoy them. More herbs are grown in the fields to be made into the potpourris, wreaths, teas, and other products that Sandy sells in her little shop. Refreshing herbal teas (like the one in the recipe on page 228) and herbal treats such as lemon balm custard and pineapple sage nut squares are served in the tearoom or the large gazebo near the herb walk.

Drawing on the experience she gained in planning and planting her gardens, Sandy advises others to "be realistic about how much time you're willing to spend on maintenance. Then lay out the space you're going to plant. Start in the middle and work toward the outer edge, planting herbs that interest you." To keep garden problems under control without pesticides, Sandy cuts out anything that is infested as soon as she spots it, and picks beetles and other large bugs off by hand and drops them into a jar of gasoline.

In the Collector's Garden, **top left,** *silvery artemisias share space with hyssops, lavender, and curry plants. The Herb Walk begins in the Colonial Garden,* **top right,** *which contains herbs our forefathers used. Marjoram,* **above left,** *and Welsh onions,* **above,** *thrive in the Culinary Garden. Simple knot patterns,* **left,** *border a path. Germander was chosen for the knot because it stays evergreen all year round. The rosemary plants are in pots so they can be dug up and taken inside during the cold winter.*

71

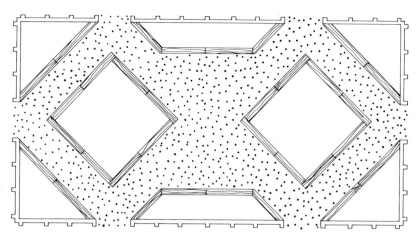

*Sandy Grieg, **left**, picks dyer's chamomile in the Dyers' Garden. The newly planted Knot Garden, **below**, is simple enough to be attempted by almost any gardener. It is traced in germander, santolina, and lavender. Thyme in full bloom, **bottom**, spills over the wooden edging in the Culinary Garden.*

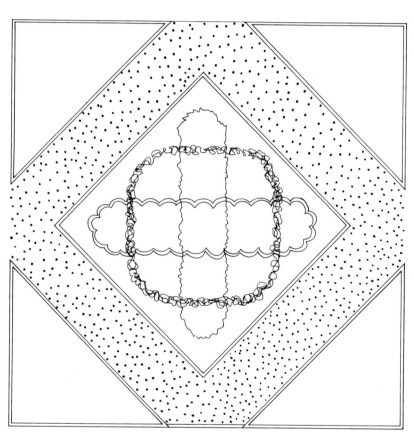

*The Bee Garden, **opposite**, is planted with herbs like bee balm, hyssop, and lavender, whose blossoms are attractive to bees. The layouts of the small gardens along the walk are as varied as the Culinary Garden, **top**, and the new Knot Garden, **above**.*

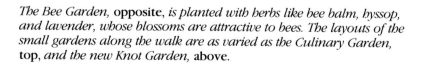

The yellow blossoms of rue, santolina, evening primrose, and lady's mantle contrast with gray artemisia and deep-purple lavender.

Jill Davies, **far left,** *checks her evening primroses. Rue in bloom,* **below far left,** *is as colorful as any perennial flower. Boughs picked for their curve,* **left,** *create an oval bed for fennel.*

THORNHAM HERBS, ENGLAND

Jill Davies, a young English herbalist, decided it was time to launch her own business when she learned that the garden at Thornham in Suffolk, England, was for sale. Surrounded by a handmade brick wall built in 1750, the former kitchen garden had been derelict since World War II. Jill and her husband cleaned the space out and started planting the crop herbs and the series of theme herb gardens that fill it today.

Trained in herbal medicine, Jill produces herbal skin and hair products and herbal teas formulated to aid relaxation and sleep, to give a gentle lift after a hard day, or to enhance well-being with vitamin-packed blends. She also often relies on herbs to cure minor ills—aloe vera to soothe burns and cuts, for example—or as a preventive measure. When Jill's baby was just a few days old, she blended some balm of gilead with glycerin and olive oil, then used it on the baby's bottom whenever she changed the diaper. The baby never suffered from diaper rash.

75

AN EXPERT'S OWN ENGLISH GARDEN

Rosemary Verey writes about gardening with the authority and knowledge gained in planning and planting the four-acre property around her lovely old stone house in England's Cotswolds. The gardens have been evolving since 1960. "To plan a garden in its entirety is very difficult," says Mrs. Verey. She feels each area should flow into the next but still reflect a change of mood. In a large garden, Mrs. Verey suggests creating vistas to draw the eye. "And a garden should look interesting in winter as well as summer," she adds.

To create a year-round garden you must rely on more than flowering plants, according to Mrs. Verey. Trees are the first bones of the garden. Interestingly shaped evergreens and shrubs are next. Early blooming trees, especially fragrant species like witch hazel, are also important, as their scent will provide pleasurable hints of summer on cold days.

At Barnsley House culinary herbs are concentrated in a pair of borders divided into diamond and triangle shapes with a low boxwood hedge. Finials of box decorate the ends. Although it's a formal arrangement, some herbs like the tall stalks of lovage tend to give the culinary garden a more casual air.

One of the latest additions to Mrs. Verey's garden is a charming and useful *potager,* a dense planting of herbs, vegetables, and flowers. The garden consists of four squares, each with its own simple symmetrical interior pattern, plans Mrs. Verey adapted from early-seventeenth-century books.

Although Mrs. Verey believes in careful planning for the garden, she enjoys the surprises, too. "I like the hazards of gardening," she says. "When a plant dies and leaves a space to be filled, put something different in to take its place."

Tall spires of mullein emphasize the lovely gates that frame the view of the temple, **above,** *beyond the pond.*

Box finials grace the ends of the formal herb garden, **left,** *that borders the path to Mrs. Verey's kitchen door. Mrs. Verey designed the traditional germander and box knots,* **top,** *to "frame the house and make an interesting graphic display in winter as well as summer." A garden seat made by Charles Verey,* **above,** *is nestled in a vine-covered arbor at one end of the* potager. *An abundantly planted barrel on the terrace,* **above right,** *is surrounded by self-sown lady's mantle. The carefully laid stone path in the* potager, **right,** *is wide enough to accommodate a wheelbarrow and is edged with lavender to attract the honeybees.*

AN AROMATIC COTSWOLDS GARDEN

I tried to take a formal design and turn it into an aromatic garden," says Guy Acloque. He has succeeded admirably. The gardens at Alderley Grange in Gloucestershire, England, are as fragrant as they are beautiful, and many of their pleasures come from herbs. "This garden is really a thing of the spirit," he says. "Walking through it is a spiritual uplift, especially in the

evening when the garden's at its most aromatic, the scent wafting through the air. Even the bees and the moths are delightful; they activate nature."

Mr. Acloque traces his fascination for herbs and aromatic plants to his early childhood in the 1940s, when he lived next door to Eleanor Sinclair-Rhode, "who had a wonderfully aromatic garden and was also the author of many interesting books on the subject. During those dark years her garden was a haven of peace and delight far removed from the perils of war."

Roses and herbs like lamb's ears, santolina, and lady's mantle lend their beauty to one of the glorious herbaceous borders at Alderley Grange, **above.** *A decorative clay pot filled with sage,* **far left,** *sits in the garden. Fragrant lavender grows in formal cement urns,* **left,** *at each corner of the lily pond.*

Lady's mantle edges the rose-filled border leading to the house, **opposite**. Fennel adds a lacy accent. The formal herb garden in one corner of the garden is surrounded by roses. The pie-shaped sections are edged with box and filled with a variety of fragrant herbs like valerian, sage, rosemary, lemon balm, and meadowsweet.

Mr. Acloque and his wife discovered Alderley in 1974. "I shall always remember the hot July day when we first saw the gardens here," he says. "We fell in love with the place and decided to buy almost immediately." For the ten years before the Acloques bought the house, Avilde Lees-Milne, the well-known English gardener and writer, and her husband had lived at Alderley and created "a magical garden within the old walls." Although he claims to have been an amateur when he took over the gardens, Mr. Acloque slowly began enlarging the collection of aromatic plants that Mrs. Milne had started. "My greatest delight was to discover the incense rose (rose primula) whose leaves give out such a wonderful smell of incense after a shower of rain," he says.

Mr. Acloque's joy in his garden is shared enthusiastically with others. To those who would like to have their own scented garden, he says, "When planning an aromatic garden, always remember to plant with profusion and never confusion. The combinations are endless and you can have hours of happiness reaping your rewards."

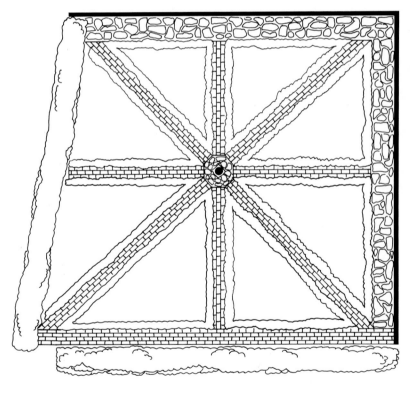

The plan of the formal herb garden, **left,** *could be adapted to a simpler planting. One of the most interesting uses of herbs in the garden is underplanting trees. In the* allée, **top,** *clove pinks, mint, thyme, strawberries, lady's mantle, and violets are planted randomly along the path. Guy Acloque grows and keeps a supply of replacement plants,* **above,** *in a small cold frame outside the greenhouse in one corner of the garden.*

Lemon balm, roses, fennel, and lady's mantle, **far left,** *are planted side by side in one section of the border. A variety of old-fashioned roses,* **top left,** *has been collected for the rose garden. Bronze fennel,* **above,** *grows undisturbed where it has self-seeded along the path. Low plantings of herbs like lady's mantle, chamomile, and violets,* **center left,** *provide a natural setting for the lily pool. Glorious masses of herbs and flowers are used for color, shape, and texture as well as scent in the border,* **bottom left.**

*The traditional sixteenth-century knot garden, **far right**, is surrounded by simple geometric beds of herbs from the period, the whole forming a patterned square. Several such squares would have been used for a large garden. Dark-green germander, golden marjoram, silvery artemisia, lavender, and pinks, **right**, illustrate how simple herbs can make a colorful garden.*

SIXTEENTH-CENTURY MUSEUM GARDEN

Patterned after books and sixteenth-century illustrations, the garden at the Tudor House Museum is as colorful and appealing as any herb garden can be. Its prototype might have existed in 1520 when Sir Richard Lyster, the Lord Chief Justice of England, went to Southampton to escape the diseases and noise of London. It's the sort of garden where, almost 500 years ago, lords and ladies might have feasted at torchlit banquets among the fragrant herbs, maids may have spread just-laundered linen over rosemary and lavender bushes to gather up the scent as it dried, and the lady of the house would have harvested herbs to distill into potpourris and potions.

A charming walled refuge, the abundantly planted garden contains only the hundred or so most commonly used herbs of the sixteenth century. Originally, about half of these were brought from Europe to England by the Romans. The rest were cultivated from the wild, rescued from fields that were being overtaken as towns got bigger, or gathered by people who sought out freak or double varieties and then swapped their seeds with others. Later, wealthy herb collectors sent to the colonies for seeds and added these exotic new varieties to the gardens.

Small versions of all the features that might have been included in a Tudor garden are reproduced at the Tudor House Museum. Any part of this garden could be successfully adapted today to even the smallest space, filling it with the same lush color and scent enjoyed by the original owners many years ago.

In Tudor times, the fountain, **top**, would have been supplied with well water or rain drained from the roof. It is surrounded by creeping thyme and lavender. Plantings of garden and red-leafed sage, lavender, pinks, and thyme, **above**, are another example of how colorful herbs can be.

85

The hedged herb garden, **above,** *has the feeling of enclosed gardens of centuries ago. The path to the garden,* **below,** *is bordered with lady's mantle, lamb's ears, and rue.*

REVIVING A MANOR HOUSE GARDEN

Henry VIII gave the original Parham Park to Robert Palmer in 1540. Now only traces of the fourteenth- and fifteenth-century buildings remain at the site of the handsome gray stone manor house and its lovely gardens. The gardens were redesigned in 1982 by Peter Coats, English garden authority and writer, with plantings that required far less labor but retained the character and atmosphere of the old gardens. Although large areas of the kitchen garden and some scattered beds were forgotten, the old walls dating from the eighteenth century or earlier survived and magnificent borders were re-created. Mr. Coats's plan for the borders is based on perennials that lend interest and color to the garden for a good part of the year rather than on labor-intensive bedding plants. The shrubs and flowers, including the many herbs, were selected for their leaf color as well as for their flowers.

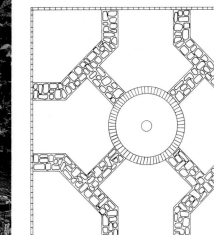

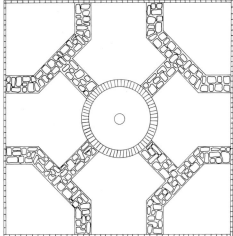

The lavender edging the rose garden, **above far left,** *adds its fragrance to the air. More lavender,* **top left,** *grows along the path to the greenhouse. Lemon balm, sage, lady's mantle, and yarrow are some of the herbs in the herbaceous border,* **below far left.** *A statue,* **above,** *is landscaped with rosemary, lady's mantle, and pinks. Rue grows in one of the unusual planters in the corners of the formal herb garden,* **bottom left.** *Marjoram grows around the base. The plan for the inner section of the garden,* **center left,** *could be changed to substitute a sundial for the pool.*

A lovely pair of wrought-iron gates frame the view of the main border. The front of the border is filled with lush plantings of lady's mantle, sage, catmint, and rue, which soften the line of the path while they suppress weeds and eliminate the chore of edging. The formal herb garden to one side of the central path is surrounded by a tall hedge, giving it the feeling of an outdoor room, an impression heightened by the English teak garden benches where visitors can sit and enjoy the setting.

ARTISTRY IN THE *POTAGER*

The Château of Villandry is surrounded by some of the most beautiful gardens in France, restored to their sixteenth-century glory through the loving care of Dr. Joachim Carvallo, a Spaniard, and his American wife. When Dr. Carvallo bought the run-down château in 1906, three distinct levels remained from earlier days to suggest the original structure. The series of exquisite gardens he created are based on this layout and his historical research of the gardens of the period.

On the topmost level, a water garden sends water to the canals and moat around the château. On the next level are two parterres. In the first, the "Garden of Love," beautifully manicured boxwood hedges are shaped into hearts and swords, their centers filled with bright flowers. The smaller parterre, situated on the other side of the canal, is a large square divided into four sections, each outlined in boxwood and filled with abstract boxwood shapes surrounded by herbs like rosemary.

But the most famous garden at Villandry is the spectacular *potager* on the lowest level. Such kitchen gardens were often

The potager *and the town beyond,* **top,** *are visible from the château. A box-edged bed,* **above,** *is planted with savory. The box hedges in the Garden of Love,* **opposite,** *are clipped into intricate designs interplanted with roses and other flowers.*

88

placed close to the château so guests could admire their vegetables and plants from faraway places. This one covers two acres and is made up of nine squares, each planted in a different pattern. The broad sand paths that separate the squares are interrupted at each intersection by a small sunken pool whose shape and burbling water recall a Moorish garden. At each corner, a bower covered with fragrant roses or jasmine provides a pleasant resting spot where visitors can enjoy the serene beauty of this kitchen garden.

As the seasons change, so does the garden, newly grown crops replacing those that are spent. Plans for the many plantings are made well in advance to ensure that the gardens will always be at their peak.

The potager, **left**, *comprises nine sections, each with its own carefully planned design. In the lower parterre,* **right**, *rosemary grows between the fancifully shaped box hedges. Topiaries line the path and petunias edge the beds in the herb garden,* **below**.

91

CONTAINER GARDENS

What could brighten a city view more than a garden of thyme, sage, and orange nasturtiums growing on a terrace outside your windows? Or add more instant charm and fragrance to a kitchen than a potted garden of chives, parsley, marjoram, and basil blooming on a windowsill or just beyond a door? Once you've seen the possibilities for planting herbs in pots and window boxes, you'll realize that you can grow an herb garden even if you have limited space, no sunlight, a yard with poor soil, or no yard at all. And container gardens have a major advantage over in-ground ones: the plants can be moved—to follow a patch of sun, escape a storm, or decorate a dinner party.

Most herbs, from a bay tree to parsley and chives, can be grown successfully in pots, so you can choose the herbs for your container garden almost as freely as you would for an in-ground garden. Even herbs with long taproots, like dill and borage, will do well if your container is deep enough. Only very tall herbs such as angelica and lovage are impractical.

Plants with invasive roots, like mint, are best grown in a pot of their own, but you can mix them with other herbs in a large container if you sink a piece of wood or metal, such as a coffee can with the top and bottom removed, around the roots when planting, or put the plant in its own smaller pot within the soil in the larger container.

Sometimes sun doesn't reach all the way to ground level in a small garden, but sunstruck shelves attached to the garden fence or the house can hold a kitchen garden in pots, **left**. *Rosemary,* **top**, *thrives in a large clay pot set in a sunny spot in the garden. At the American Museum in Britain, potted bay trees,* **above**, *trained as standards, decorate the terrace. A Nantucket herb garden,* **right**, *blooms in pots arranged on the sunny steps that lead up to the house.*

The portable herb gardens, **above left**, *were made by Joe Ruggiero, who added handles and legs to old nursery flats. They can be moved to take advantage of the sun, retreat to the kitchen when cold weather arrives, or double as a centerpiece for an informal* supper. A group of potted herb plants, **above right**, *clustered in an attractive container like this footbath, will serve as a table decoration. Most herbs can be grown successfully in pots,* **below**, *and are decorative as well as useful.*

IN THE GARDEN

Growing herbs in pots and boxes outdoors allows you greater flexibility in the design of your garden. You can add color and texture in spots where it's impractical to dig a garden, put your herbs exactly where you want them, and grow plants that need sun where it's sunny, and those that like a little shade where they'll have it. You can soften the straight lines of a patio or path with a scattering of pots or use them to add height where it's needed. And because potted plants are so portable, you can rearrange them frequently or gather them all together for an impressive party display. In considering your design, think of groupings of small pots just as you would a bed of plants, and use large pots to focus attention on areas you want to highlight.

Preparing Your Pot for Planting

Good drainage is as important in container gardening as it is for planting in the ground, so make sure your pot has drainage holes in the bottom—from one for a small pot up to eight or nine for anything as large as a barrel. Cover the bottom of the pot with a layer of broken crockery or pebbles to aid drainage and contain the soil. A small pot will need just a few

A half barrel planted with sage, **above far left,** *provides an abundant harvest. Another barrel,* **top left,** *holds a compact kitchen garden. A planter filled with houseleeks,* **top right,** *is the focal point of a garden. Ingredients for an Italian dinner—tomatoes, basil, parsley, and oregano— grow in this barrel,* **above left.** *An old stone sink set on a column,* **above right,** *holds sage at Parham Park. Creeping thyme,* **left,** *cascades over a clay pot at the National Arboretum.*

The well-clipped shapes of the bay and myrtle on the patio of Lady Somerset's country house are enhanced by the size and shape of their pots.

bits of crockery, but if you're using a large container, layer the bottom with at least 2 inches of crockery or pebbles. Set an extra-large container like a barrel in place before filling it; using perlite or a similar material for the bottom third of the planting material will make it lighter and easier to move if necessary. Finally, add soil to within 1 inch of the top of the pot. Almost every container, including hanging pots and window boxes, should be prepared this way.

The one exception is a hanging wire basket, which you should line with damp sphagnum moss. If you want to plant hanging herbs in the side of the basket, poke holes in the moss and insert the roots of the plants before filling the basket with potting soil. Burying a clump of moss in the center of the pot will help retain moisture.

Potting Soil

You can pamper container-grown herbs with good, friable soil that you buy from your garden center or mix yourself. If you're planning to use a large amount of soil, it will be more economical to mix it yourself. You'll need good loam, compost or peat, and builder's sand or perlite—all available at a garden center. The best formula for most plants is 3 parts loam, 1 part compost or peat, and 1 part builder's sand or perlite. You can vary this mixture to suit special needs: 1 spoonful of lime can be added for herbs that prefer an alkaline soil, for instance, or more peat can be used for those that prefer damp soil.

General Care for Potted Herbs

Herbs requiring full sun need at least 5 to 6 hours of sunlight a day to grow into healthy plants, indoors or out. If you don't have a spot that offers that much sun, concentrate on herbs like mint, lemon balm, bay, parsley, and thyme that can get along on a little less; or use lights indoors.

Potted plants dry out faster than those planted in the garden, and so must be kept well watered. Overwatering, however, is just as bad for herbs as letting them dry out completely; check the soil and water when the top inch is dry. During the hottest part of the summer, this may mean watering every day. Don't rely on rainstorms to water for you outdoors: if the potted herbs have heavy foilage, the soil may not receive sufficient water.

Although heavy fertilization interferes with the full development of an herb's fragrance, potted herbs, without the earth's nutrients to draw on, must be fed regularly. A diluted organic fertilizer applied once a month should be sufficient.

As with any potted plant, replenish the soil in your herb pots occasionally and change it completely every two or three years. With good care, container-grown herbs can be as fragrant, as flavorful, and as beautiful as herbs grown in the earth; even with the best care, though, don't expect potted herbs to grow as large as they would in the garden.

ON CITY TERRACES

You can thank containers for one of the city's most amazing and delightful sights: look twenty stories up the face of a forbidding brick building, or over miles of gray rooftops, and suddenly there's a lush, green garden far above the earth. Planting a garden on a city terrace, nothing more than a patch of stone, wouldn't be possible without containers.

More and more of these city gardens include herbs. Peter Dunlop, a New York City landscape architect, started growing and selling herbs in 1983 after customers asked for them at his plant shop, Horticulture House. As the demand increased, he built a greenhouse in the country, then a second one. Now so many of his clients grow herbs, Peter has other nurserymen

helping him meet the demand for starter plants.

"The key thing in terrace gardening is water," Peter says. "You have to realize container gardening is false gardening. Your herbs aren't rooted in Mother Earth, where even if the soil dries down to a depth of two or three inches, there's still moisture below. When you've got herbs in containers, the sun is baking them from the bottom up, the sides in, and the top down." Wind increases the problem of dryness in a terrace garden. "But all the watering you have to do makes fertilizing important, too," he adds. "As the water drains through the containers, the fertilizer drains with it." When you're watering each day or two, he recommends feeding your plants every three weeks.

Herbs thrive in window boxes overlooking the city, **above,** *when they are watered conscientiously and frequently fed.*

*Herbs grown in small pots, **left**, can be moved to catch available sun. Peter Dunlop uses specially made galvanized boxes in the terrace gardens he designs. Because substantial labor is involved in bringing soil and plants to the terrace, he makes much of the planting permanent, including perennial herbs like sage and thyme, **above**.*

97

IN THE HOUSE

M any culinary herbs thrive on a sunny windowsill, and
you can even grow a big pot of fringed lavender or pots
of scented geraniums to sweeten the air in your house.
To cultivate herbs successfully indoors, find a spot where they
will get from 4 to 5 hours of good sunlight every day, preferably
with a southern or western exposure, or 8 to 10 hours of
artificial light. Turn the plants occasionally so they will grow
evenly as they reach toward the light source.

Your herbs will do well in an energy-conscious environ-
ment with daytime temperatures about 68°. Since herbs don't
like extremes of heat and cold, don't allow temperatures to
remain above 70° or to drop below 55° at night, and be sure the
plants are protected from drafts and positioned away from
radiators. Keep them far enough apart so that air will be able to
circulate around them freely to help prevent bugs and disease.
If you find bugs on the plants, hold your hand over the soil, turn
the pot upside down, and swish the foliage through soapy water,
or spray with an insecticide soap. Avoid chemical preparations
for herbs you're going to eat.

Use regular potting soil or a soilless mix, and feed the
plants with a diluted organic fertilizer on a regular 2-week
schedule during the winter, a bit less frequently during the
summer. Water your herbs when they need it. It could be as
frequently as every other day, but will vary with your house
temperature and the amount of humidity in the air.

Since indoor herbs are not as hardy as those growing in
the garden, harvest just the tip of a stem or a leaf here and there
rather than cutting the plants back as you would outdoors.

Grouping several plants together, **opposite far left,** *increases humidity in the atmosphere. A tin lining can turn any box into a waterproof container. Thyme, rosemary, and marjoram,* **opposite left,** *grow under the skylight. Given the proper growing conditions, lemon,* **top,** *and other scented geraniums are excellent houseplants. Antiques dealer Marston Luce uses a rosemary bush, usually kept near a window, in a table arrangement,* **above.** *Herbs and flowers are gathered in an indoor country garden,* **left,** *by a city window. Marston Luce lets thyme hide the soil around a calla lily,* **right.**

Many herbs can be grown indoors if they are given the proper care. Containers can range from antique pitchers and pots to classic terra-cotta planters.

THE VICTOR M

HERBAL DECORATIONS

*O*ne of the greatest joys of growing herbs is using the harvest to decorate your house, bringing the color, beauty, and scents of your garden indoors.

In summer you can set bouquets of mint on your windowsills, where breezes will pick up their fresh scent and carry it throughout the house. Sprigs of herbs in every shade of green, every texture, will spice a country bouquet; fresh herbs and delicate herb flowers can be tucked into a small twig wreath to put around a hurricane lamp or a group of candles on the table. And for

Herbs and flowers, **left,** *hang from the rafters of an old barn to dry. Arranged in an indoor window box,* **above left,** *they are a cheery remembrance of summer during gray winter days. A straw hat,* **above right,** *banded with dried herbs and flowers, can be worn or used for decoration.*

103

Bouquets and pomanders are two of the many ways designer Robert K. Lewis uses herbs in his Long Island home.

a hands-on lobster dinner, float leaves of lemon-scented geranium or lemon verbena in finger bowls.

You can string bunches of lavender and hang them at your windows for fresh, clean-smelling country "curtains," or use delicate herbal flowers and fragrant leaves to fashion wreaths and bou-

quets for every room. And with patience, a young myrtle or rosemary plant can be trained into the shape of a tree to give a simple elegance to rooms and table settings.

When the snow is falling, potpourri you've blended from leaves and favorite flowers will re-

*A basket of dried herbs and flowers, **far left**, can add color and warmth to your house year round, while potpourri, **above left**, adds fresh fragrance. Delicately colored, perfectly dried roses, **left**, accent Norma Jean Lathrop's German statice wreath. The herbal sachets in the Shaker basket, **above**, have been made with bits of old fabric.*

call the scent and beauty of your summer garden. Small bunches of aromatic herbs can hang in closets, or sachets can be slipped among your linens. At Christmas, the spicy aroma of pomanders can fill the house and herbs can be fashioned into colorful wreaths, everlasting trees, and nosegays to use as sweet-smelling ornaments.

Decorating with herbs increases the many pleasures you get from your garden, keeping its beauty alive indoors as well as out, in cold weather as well as warm.

Harvesting the Crop

To enjoy the rewards of your garden indoors year round, it's essential that you harvest herbs properly.

The best time to pick herbs is on a clear day, as soon as the dew dries but before the sun's heat dissipates the essential oils that give them their scent. If you're harvesting herbs for fragrance, try to pick them just before they bloom, when they're at their most aromatic. If for flowers, pick them soon after the buds open, before the petals start to fade and brown.

Drying Herbs in Bunches

To dry long-stemmed herbs—like the mints, southernwood and other artemisias, yarrow, and goldenrod—gather them into small bunches, tie the ends together with string, and hang the bunches upside down in a dim place and far enough apart so air will circulate between them.

They can be hung from the beams in the ceiling of a well-ventilated basement or attic; in an old barn or drying shed if you're lucky enough to have one; or from beams or wall pegs in an airy room. If you hang herbs in the kitchen, keep them away from the stove and sink, where steam may interfere with drying.

Racks are an alternative to the ceiling for hanging herbs. You can use antique or reproduction herb drying racks, old laundry racks, swivel towel racks, or blanket stands. You can also make your own drying rack; it's a matter of simple carpentry and copying a picture of one you like. Or tie the herb bunches to a clothes hanger hung on a rod or hook.

Drying Leaves and Petals

To dry leaves and petals individually—rose petals, scented geraniums, or lemon verbena, for example—or whole flowerheads without the stems, scatter them in a single layer on

The head of an old rake, **above,** *is used as a decorative drying rack. Chive blossoms for wreaths and arrangements,* **left,** *are supported by a piece of screening to dry. A bowl of potpourri,* **above right,** *waits to be scooped into individual containers. Norma Jean Lathrop dries lavender sticks and other herbs and flowers from her California garden,* **right,** *on a simple screen. In London, florist Kenneth Turner creates a miniature forest,* **far right,** *with dried curry plants and dried branches.*

a drying tray. Drying trays are available from herb shops or you can make your own by stretching muslin, nylon screening, or netting tightly over a simple wooden frame; you can also use a sweater dryer, a shallow basket, or a clean window screen propped on bricks. If you need to save space, use trays that can be stacked.

Whichever method you select, the leaves will dry fastest if the air is able to circulate around them on all sides. Drying time varies from 2 to 10 days, depending on the humidity in the air and the moisture in the leaves and flowers. If damp weather slows down the drying process too much, you might want to spread the herbs on a cookie sheet and finish drying them in an oven set at the *lowest* temperature and with the door left ajar so moisture can escape. They're ready when the leaves are crisp and brittle. The faster the leaves and flowers dry, the more color and fragrance they'll retain.

HERBS AS A WAY OF LIFE

So diverse are the uses of herbs, so seductive their pleasures, that what starts as a limited interest often turns into a consuming avocation. Like many others, Barbara Ohrbach in New York and Emily Carter in Virginia, each in her own way, have turned that avocation into a rewarding way of life.

Emily Carter, **above**, *gathers field-grown yarrow.*

Simple bouquets, **far left,** *look more important when several are grouped together. Barbara Orbach uses similar containers to add impact. Herbs dry on a handmade twig rack,* **top left,** *in the Carters' kitchen. Barbara Ohrbach's neatly labeled herb vinegars,* **center left,** *are lined up behind part of her collection of old herbals. The rustic basket of dried thyme twigs,* **bottom left,** *is filled with dried dittany of Crete.*

109

On weekends, Barbara Ohrbach harvests herbs in the garden of her converted carriage house. Creeping thyme grows between the slates on the patio, adding its fragrance to the air when someone walks across it.

A PASSION FOR HERBAL SCENTS

Barbara Ohrbach began collecting early herbals and old books on plants and flowers as a hobby, searching them out in bookstores and flea markets every time her job with a fashion magazine took her to Europe. "Reading them was almost like a course in the daily life of the times," she says. As her interest grew, so did her collection, expanding to include English and American books on housekeeping and manners dating from 1790 to 1910, a period when homemakers used the fresh fragrance of sweet-smelling herbs to scent rooms, freshen closets, and chase moths.

Fascinated by the recipes in her books and by the potpourris she saw being sold in small shops all over Europe, Barbara decided to make some potpourri of her own. Friends were so enthusiastic about the results that Barbara and her husband, Mel, a fashion industry executive, gave up their successful careers to open Cherchez, an inviting store filled with beautifully packaged potpourris, herbal wreaths, bunches of dried herbs and flowers, and the Victorian linens Barbara

Charming little moth bouquets, **above,** *made of German statice and moth-repellent herbs like lavender and southernwood, hang on the closet door.*

111

Spicy pomanders, **top**, are always in the making at the Ohrbachs'. Apples (you can substitute oranges if you prefer) are studded with whole cloves, then rolled in a mixture of equal parts of powdered cinnamon, nutmeg, cloves, and orris root and left to dry. Completed pomanders, **above**, are often heaped in a bowl of lavender, filling the room with a pungent fragrance. Bunches of herbs, **right**, are dried on an antique Shaker rack.

112

Freshly picked herbs are gathered in antique baskets, then made into fresh bouquets and vinegars or dried for later use.

adores. Not surprisingly, the original Cherchez potpourris were inspired by her old recipes: Rondilitia, taken from a sixteenth-century Spanish recipe; Old English Rose from an eighteenth-century recipe; and Field Flower, a Victorian fragrance reminiscent of a lush English nosegay.

Today, in addition to the New York store, Cherchez has expanded to encompass a thriving wholesale and mail-order business, as well as a small cottage industry to supply the inventory.

Although herbs are a business for the Ohrbachs, the herb garden at their country house north of New York City is a personal one. "It's just for us to enjoy," insists Barbara. Five years ago when the Ohrbachs bought the converted carriage house, there was no garden. The most logical place to plant one seemed to be the cement-covered area in front of the old carriage-house doors where the ground was flat and the sun

shone most of the day unimpeded by the old trees on the property. All the cement was laboriously broken up and the heavy chunks carted away. Then soil and sand were trucked in to create the two simple **L**-shaped beds where informally planted herbs now flourish.

Almost all the varieties of herbs in the garden are dried for wreaths and many for the bowls of fragrant potpourri that appear throughout the house. Sage, one of Barbara's favorites, is also used in fresh and dried bouquets and serves as seasoning for foods; southernwood, mugwort, and wormwood are dried to make pungent moth deterrents for closets and armoires; and lavender is often just heaped in bowls for its fragrance and beauty. Because green plants are impractical in a weekend house, the Ohrbachs arrange big bunches of dried herbs in jugs and baskets instead. In the summertime, the house is also filled with bouquets of fresh herbs.

113

CRAFTS FROM THE HARVEST

Emily Carter grew up sharing her mother's delight in collecting different varieties of herbs to plant in the garden that you saw on pages 60–61, so it's not surprising that five years ago when she decided to begin a business of her own, she chose herbs. Although the Carters' herb garden is large by most standards, it couldn't provide enough material for the plants and wreaths Emily hoped to sell, so the first year she planted over a half acre of lavender, yarrow, and catnip in the open fields close to the family house. Luckily her large family was willing to help.

All the plants were started from seed in the greenhouse. Because Emily had gotten a late start, the herbs weren't ready to be set out until July, when the intense heat can threaten delicate seedlings. Emily remembers with a mixture of love and exhaustion the hot July day when all nine Carter children had returned to Virginia for a family gathering. They took to the

Indoor winter window boxes, **left,** *are twig baskets filled with subtly colored dried herbs and flowers. They rest on the window sash, held in place with a piece of string nailed to either side of the window frame. Emily Carter,* **above,** *makes wreaths in the great hall at Muskettoe Pointe Farm.*

115

fields to set each of the carefully nurtured seedlings in place. That they grew is due to the constant watering and care Emily, assisted by her family, gave them. Now, although she still starts many of the plants from seed in the greenhouse near the house, she supplements the seedlings by propagating cuttings from the field-grown plants.

Since that first year, two additional acres of herbs have been planted. They are filled with thyme, chives, lemon balm, sage, wormwood, rue, statice, strawflowers, globe amaranth, more lavender and yarrow, and other perennials Emily uses in her wreaths. Although Emily takes pleasure in gardening, she enjoys using the herbs ornamentally even more. The Carter house is testimony to the instinctive talent that Emily and her mother, Pat, have for devising ways to use the herbs they grow.

For now, the business is based primarily on miniature and full-sized wreaths made from the harvest, which are sold at the farm, at crafts fairs, and sometimes in large quantities to companies that use them as gifts. However, Emily and Mrs. Carter plan to expand their endeavors to include a mail-order catalogue and a garden shop in one of the outbuildings, where they will serve tea.

116

The harvest, **above,** *is worked into herb wreaths and arrangements. Part of the lavender harvest is tied into small bunches and hung on string at the window,* **left,** *as a fragrant "country curtain." More lavender,* **right,** *is arranged in an antique basket.*

THE MANY WAYS OF WREATHS

Probably the best-known herbal decoration, herb wreaths offer enormous potential for individual expression. Although untold numbers of these wreaths are made every year, each is unique, reflecting the personality of the maker in its size, shape, and materials.

In the hills of western Connecticut, antiques dealer Holly Meier grows silver king artemisia and other herbs, then dries them on her antique racks before turning them into potpourris and wreaths. Holly's wreaths reflect her love for the simplicity of early country interiors. Sparse rather than lush, the wreaths are generally made of one or two common herbs like marjoram or thyme. Thinner wreaths are simply small bunches of herbs carefully overlapped, each bunch attached to the preceding one with florist's wire. For more substantial wreaths, Holly wires the herbs to a grapevine wreath base.

Holly Meier, **opposite top,** *gathers herbs for her country wreaths. She also dries a wide variety of herbs and flowers,* **opposite bottom,** *for potpourris and cooking. Part of the harvest is hung from Holly's collection of antique drying racks,* **left.** *A selection of Holly's simple but charming herb wreaths,* **right,** *are displayed on the stair well. Bouquets garnis— bundles of fresh parsley, thyme, marjoram, and bay—are dried on an antique rack in front of the fire,* **below right,** *then used to flavor soups and stews.*

Helene Lewand Koch, on the other hand, makes good use of Maine's short summers to grow fields of herbs and flowers to turn into wreaths that are more feminine, less austere than Holly's. Even the drying is done with a certain exuberance: every inch of the ceiling beams in the house where Helene and her husband, Dana, live is hung with colorful bunches of dried blossoms, reminders of summer gardens when the cold winds bluster outside.

Starting with a simple wire wreath base, Helene covers it with moss, then wires on small individual bouquets of dried green herbs, yarrow and other colorful dried flowers, and the baby's breath that gives her wreaths a lovely laciness. But no matter what combination of colors, herbs, and flowers she uses, each wreath captures the same romantic mood.

120

Field-grown herbs and flowers, **opposite top,** *provide a rich array of materials for delicate wreaths like these,* **opposite bottom.** *Symbols of the extremes of Maine's weather, summery wreaths and bouquets and a woodstove and snowshoes,* **far left,** *share space in the kitchen of Black Rock Farm. Helene and Dana Koch with their friend Karen James,* **left,** *stand in the workroom surrounded by their harvest. Delphiniums,* **above,** *hang to dry in the attic.*

121

One of the pleasures of making an herb wreath, **above,** *is choosing the colors, materials, and textures.* **Opposite,** *Norma Jean Lathrop decorates a heart-shaped wreath,* **top left,** *with dried roses. Wreaths like Norma Jean's subtly colored one of lavender and dittany of Crete,* **top center,** *can be used around a candle. Betsy Williams's Christmas wreath,* **top right,** *includes yarrow, bayberry, rosemary, coriander, thyme, rue, and lavender. Glory Condon's bay wreath,* **center left,** *and Leslie Gordon's savory wreath with garlic and pepper,* **center,** *and her thyme wreath,* **center right,** *are useful in the kitchen. Maria Price has a talent for mixing colors and textures. For a tawny autumn wreath,* **bottom left,** *she uses yarrow, santolina buds, rose hips, curry plant, strawflowers, and bits of lavender. Her bridal wreath,* **bottom center,** *is pale and delicate, with a small bag of lavender at the bottom. Maria has captured the clear colors of a summer garden,* **bottom right,** *with lamb's ears, lavender, santolina, artemisias, lily of the valley, yarrow, roses, mint, and other herbs and flowers.*

How to Make an Herb Wreath

Herb wreaths are easy and fun to make and are ideal for presents to give to special friends. Once you've mastered the basic technique, you can be as creative as you like. Look at some of the wreaths here and in the chapter "An Herbal Christmas," then let the plants in your garden and your mood dictate the design.

1. Buy a simple wire ring frame of the desired size from your florist or florist supply shop. Remember, the finished wreath will be several inches bigger than the frame by the time you've added the herbs.

2. Gather together a good supply of the herb you're planning to use as the base. Although you can use dried herbs, they're rather fragile and must be handled carefully. It's easier to work with fresh material that can be shaped to the frame as you go and will dry that way. You can pick the herbs in late summer or early fall when they are ready to be harvested and complete the basic wreath then. If you like, the wreath can be left to dry in a cool, dimly lit place with good air circulation and decorated later. Silver king artemisia is an ideal herb to start with, but santolina, thyme, lavender, lamb's ears, or any other herbs will do, as long as it's available in sufficient quantity and can be cut in pieces long enough to be wired to the frame.

3. Spread a bunch of herbs over the frame, carefully covering the wire. Overlap the bunches so that the stems of the previous bunch do not show. If the stem of the herb has a natural curve, let it follow the curve of the frame. If the stem is straight, just make sure the pieces are aligned with the frame and not sticking out at angles. Using florist's wire, attach each bunch of herbs firmly to the frame. This will be the base on which the rest of the wreath is built.

4. Once the base has been completed, take smaller pieces of the same herb and tuck them all around the inner and outer edges, with all sprigs going in the same direction.

5. Start filling in the top side of the wreath. Use more of the basic herb, alternating it with sprigs of another color or texture if you choose.

6. Now it's time to decorate the basic wreath with dried flowers like yarrow, lavender, globe amaranth, goldenrod, statice, and celosia, or the smaller, more delicate flowers of culinary herbs like chives, marjoram, mint, and sage. Dried seed pods and berries are also attractive; or you can attach cinnamon sticks or even little bags of dried herbs and spices by wiring them to florist's picks, then sticking them into the wreath or gluing the bags or sticks directly to the top layer of herbs with a glue gun.

An alternative method of wreath making uses simple grapevine, honeysuckle, or wisteria vine as a base for the herbs. To start, form a circle with three thicknesses of vine. Once you

have the basic circle, continue wrapping the vine in and out around the circle. When you reach the end of one piece of vine, tuck the end under one of the strands already in place in the wreath; start the next piece by catching its end in the wreath the same way.

After the wreath has reached the desired thickness, tuck in, wire on, or glue on the decorative herbs and flowers. Although the base can be completely covered, letting some of the unadorned vine show through will add to the rustic charm of the finished wreath.

A straw wreath form from the florist is another possible wreath base. You can wire bunches of the background herbs around the base or attach them with florist's pins stuck into the straw. Decorative material should be attached with pins or glue

Helene Koch combines dried flowers from her farm with rosemary, santolina, lavender, and sage for a wreath, **opposite,** *that looks like a garden in full bloom. A potpourri wreath,* **left,** *from Meadowsweet Herb Farm in Vermont mixes the soft greens of lamb's ears, artemisias, bay, and other dried herbs with the pinks*

and purples of roses and flowers. Cinnamon sticks add more fragrance. Helene's bridal wreath, **top,** *combines a variety of herbs with pale flowers and baby's breath for a romantic look.*

125

POTPOURRI'S PLEASURES

In Elizabethan cottages and castles, potpourris, aromatic mixtures of dried leaves and flowers, had an essential purpose: they sweetened air that was musty and ill-smelling from damp weather and primitive sanitation conditions. Today, although potpourris still mask mustiness and household odors, their primary purpose is pleasure—the pleasure of a gently perfumed room that evokes memories of the fragrant blooms of summer even during a winter storm.

Piled into small bowls or jars and placed throughout the house, the delicately tinted leaves and petals are as pretty as they are fragrant. But you needn't stop there. You can layer different-colored petals in a clear glass vase, using them to anchor the stems of dried flowers or leaves. You can make potpourri balls or animals by covering forms—a styrofoam ball or a plastic toy animal—with a thick layer of glue and then rolling them in potpourri. Sachets filled with potpourri can scent a closet or drawer. Or pillows stuffed with potpourri can add a special dimension to a bed or chair, releasing their lovely fragrance when you settle in.

Traditionally, potpourris are based on the fragrance of roses, but other scented flowers like jasmine, peonies, and pinks can be used as well. Almost any kind of nonfragrant flower can be added for color. The flower petals are mixed with dried aromatic leaves from herbs such as lavender and scented geraniums, then powdered spices like cinnamon and cloves or the fragrant seeds of herbs like anise can be added in small amounts if desired. A fixative (generally orris root or gum benzoin) will help blend the scent and prolong its life. A few drops of the essential oil from a flower, herb, or spice can be stirred in for accent. For a more complex perfume, mix in whole spices, dried orange or lemon peel, and chips of woods like sandalwood or cedar.

You can also give potpourris a woodsy smell with pine needles; the scent of freshly cut hay with woodruff; a spicy smell with cinnamon; a citrus tang with lemon balm, lemon verbena, lemon thyme, or dried citrus peel; or an exotic aroma with sandalwood, vetiver, or patchouli.

If you've never made potpourri, start with a recipe from a current volume on potpourri making or an old stillroom book. Stillroom books—named for the room where housewives 100 years ago or more kept herbs, dried flowers, and a still for drawing out essential oils—contain recipes for potpourris, cosmetics, soaps, and even medicines. Original stillroom books are rare antiques now, but you can find reproductions of the recipes or updated versions.

Emily Carter, **left,** *harvests lavender for her potpourris and wreaths. A heart-shaped frame,* **top,** *has been covered with potpourri. The old-fashioned roses,* **center,** *from Maria Price's garden are dried for their beauty and scent. Potpourri,* **bottom,** *can be as colorful as it is fragrant.*

127

Once you've mastered the basic procedure, experiment by dividing one flower-and-leaf mixture into three or four equal portions, then adding different spices, fixatives, and oils to each. Keep good records of what you've done so you will be able to reproduce any scent you particularly like.

In addition to using a fixative, a potpourri's scent will last much longer if the mixture is stored in a covered jar and the lid removed only when you're in the room. Loose potpourri in bowls and baskets is often more appealing, however, and although the fragrance will fade more quickly, it can easily be revived by adding a few drops of the essential oil.

How to Make Potpourri

Here are the guidelines for making a good potpourri.

1. When picking flowers and leaves, select only perfect ones. Flowers should be cut just after they open, but you can pick those that are a bit past their prime if you carefully remove any petals that have started to turn brown. Avoid using flowers that have been sprayed with chemicals.

2. Dry the flowers and herbs according to the directions on pages 106–7. They must be absolutely dry or the potpourri will mold. Dry the flowers you're using for color only, like zinnias and cosmos, separately in silica gel, since they tend to lose their color when dried in bunches. The gel is available at florist supply stores and directions for using it are on the box.

3. Once the harvest is dried, store each kind of flower and leaf separately. Label the jars: it's amazing how much alike leaves can look after they're dried.

4. When you are ready to make the potpourri, use only a

London florist Kenneth Turner layers lavender and potpourri in a tall glass cylinder, **top left,** *to anchor a bouquet of dried flowers. The ceiling of Helene Koch's house is covered with fragrant and nonfragrant flowers,* **top,** *that add color to her potpourris and wreaths. For a pretty alternative to a bowl of* *potpourri, make one of Barbara Ohrbach's scented potpourri balls,* **above.** *Cover a styrofoam ball with a thick layer of white glue, then roll it in potpourri. Keep the fragrance at its peak by occasionally adding a drop of scented oil. Just-picked lavender and yarrow,* **right,** *sit on a bench in the Carters' garden.*

128

glass or ceramic bowl to mix ingredients and stir only with your hands or a wooden spoon. Metal utensils affect the aroma.

5. After you're satisfied with the scent and look of the potpourri, put it in an airtight container and let it sit in a cool, dark place for several weeks while the fragrance mellows. Shake the container occasionally.

TWO POTPOURRI POTIONS

Elizabeth Walker's Meadow Herbs is a family-run cottage industry in a little country town in the south of England that makes herb pillows and sachets, herbal oils and cosmetics, and a wide range of potpourris. The potpourri blends are based on adaptations of traditional recipes that Elizabeth researched or created for special purposes inspired by traditional folklore interpretations of the curative and magical properties of herbs. Herbs like valerian and hops, although not markedly sweet-smelling, are thought to be extremely sedative. Others, like marjoram, chamomile, and lemon verbena, are said to soothe the nerves. Sweet smells are supposed to be aphrodisiac.

Here are two of Elizabeth's recipes: one to stimulate thoughts of love, the other to encourage sleep. While there's no guarantee that they'll work, there's no harm—and lots of fun—in trying.

Elizabeth Walker experiments with carefully measured amounts of various ingredients, **above,** *to create her delightful potpourris. Adapt Kenneth Turner's decorative idea and fill a tall glass jar,* **right,** *with layers of potpourri, dried herbs, leaves, and flowers.*

QUIET SLEEP POTPOURRI

To be placed in a bowl in the bedroom.

- 2 cups rosemary flowers and leaves (said to dispel nightmares)
- 2 cups lavender flowers (to dispel melancholy)
- 1 cup chamomile flowers (to soothe the nerves)
- 2 tablespoons marjoram (to act as a sedative)
- ½ tablespoon aniseed (for scent)
- ½ tablespoon powdered orris root
- 6 drops bergamot oil

This mixture can be made to look more substantial, or to fill a large bowl, with the addition of lemon verbena leaves, colored petals, or linden flowers.

LOVERS' POTPOURRI

- 2 cups peony petals (for its sweet smell, said to be an aphrodisiac)
- 1 cup rosebuds (the flowers of love)
- 1 cup chamomile flowers (to soothe the nerves)
- 1 cup linden flowers (for its relaxing power)
- 1 tablespoon allspice (for scent)
- 4 to 5 drops of the best patchouli oil available Flowers of forget-me-not for decoration

A little more oil can be added, but too much is overpowering rather than aphrodisiac. Jasmine flowers can replace, or supplement, the rosebuds.

AN HERBAL BOUQUET

Herbal bouquets are as varied as the people who arrange them and the gardens from which they're picked. Sometimes the herbs are no more than a fragrant green background for other flowers; sometimes the herbs themselves are the flowers; and sometimes they are just a subtle bunch of contrasting greens and textures. The container contributes to the finished effect, too. The same unsophisticated handful of herbs that looks fresh and natural in a simple white jug can be imposing in an elegant bowl or vase.

Pat Braun, owner of Salou, one of New York's most innovative florists, was first attracted by the simplicity of herbs. Now he uses them in arrangements the way he would any flower.

"My philosophy," he says, "is that a bouquet should be simple enough for each flower to be seen." The tiny herb bouquets he sometimes creates for an informal table setting are a good example of this approach. "I began making individual bouquets to solve the problem of how to put flowers on an antique table forty feet long and so narrow there was no room for a centerpiece," he explained. It's an idea that could be adopted by anyone.

The wonderful bonus of an herb bouquet, of course, is its fragrance. Imagine the delightfully lemony smell of balm or the refreshing scent of mint perfuming the house. And herb bouquets can be useful, too: just snip a flavorful leaf for instant seasoning right at the table.

A country table, **above,** *is set with Pat Braun's herb bouquets. The bouquets,* **left,** *contain waxflower, forget-me-not, rosemary, mint, lemon sage, santolina, German statice, eucalyptus, parsley, and scented geranium.*

The delicate sprigs of flowering mint, **above,** *are perfectly suited to Robert K. Lewis's antique English creamware quintal flower horn. Bright-gold flowering dill,* **right,** *makes a simple country bouquet. The clusters of fresh herbs in the Carters' kitchen,* **far right,** *are handy to snip for seasoning.*

Lady Caroline Somerset contrasts
the bright blue of delphinium,
lush sprays of golden-green lady's
mantle, and velvety gray lamb's
ears, **left,** in an elegant bouquet
for the drawing room of her
country house. The dramatically
shaped stalks of lamb's ears,
above, with their tiny purple
flowers and downy gray-green
leaves, make a striking bouquet.

135

ELIZABETHAN NOSEGAYS

In Elizabethan England, people carried and sniffed tussie-mussies—little nosegays of aromatic herbs and flowers—to help disguise the dreadful stench of London's streets. These serviceable bouquets often included herbs thought to be disinfectants, like lavender, rosemary, and rue, as protection from the plague and other diseases.

By the Victorian era, highly stylized nosegays had become a favorite way to send messages to friends and lovers. Each herb and flower had its own accepted definition: lemon balm meant sympathy, for instance; chervil was for sincerity; rue conveyed disdain; parsley represented festivity; roses were for love; and sweet violets stood for modesty. The practice undoubtedly led to an occasional misunderstanding, however, as some herbs have double meanings: basil, for example, can symbolize both love and hate.

These nosegays still offer lovely possibilities for using the herbs from your garden. Displayed fresh in a water-filled vase or

Herbs and flowers at the American Museum in Britain, **right,** *are made into fresh tussie-mussies, old-fashioned bouquets of fragrant herbs and flowers. A volunteer,* **left,** *shows museum visitors how to make a tussie-mussie. The finished tussie-mussies,* **below,** *are among the most popular items in the museum's gift shop*

Freshly cut herbs and flowers, **far left,** *from the museum garden fill a trug. Helene Koch uses some of her dried herbs and flowers for more traditional tussie-mussies like this bridal bouquet,* **left.**

dried in a vase without water, they add color and fragrance to even the smallest corner of the house, and they also make very special gifts, especially for someone confined by illness. The fragrance will freshen and, if the Elizabethans can be believed, may even disinfect the air of a sick room.

As a bridal bouquet, a tussie-mussie can be both pretty and symbolic, offering Victorian messages of love (rosebuds), remembrance (rosemary), purity (mint), courage (thyme), the return of happiness (lily of the valley), and luck (lavender), and even a touch of Victorian ambiguity, as lavender also stands for distrust.

Fresh tussie-mussies, more freely styled and with a greater variety of flowers and colors than the Victorian versions, are among the most popular gifts in the Herb Shop at the American Museum in Britain in Bath, England. The museum, created to show how British traditions were adapted to suit rustic life in colonial America, is in a lovely old manor house furnished with American antiques and surrounded by gardens. There is a traditionally designed garden planted with herbs the colonists brought from England as well as some they were given by the Indians, a rose and flower garden modeled on George Washington's at Mount Vernon, and a garden for plants employed for dyeing.

The American Museum's staff gives regular demonstrations on tussie-mussie making. Here are instructions, based on those in a museum booklet, for creating one of the nosegays.

138

How to Make a Tussie-Mussie

You can make tussie-mussies with fresh herbs and flowers or with dried materials. A fresh tussie-mussie can be dried with its charm and fragrance intact if you're careful to use only those fresh ingredients that dry easily: lavender, thyme, mint, rosemary, and southernwood, for example. Use as many sweet-smelling herbs as possible, and try to include herbs with contrasting colors and leaf shapes. These simple guidelines will yield a traditional tussie-mussie.

1. Start with a fresh rose, still in bud, or a few sprigs of a flowering herb like sage. Surround the rose or flowering herb with a circle of green-leafed herb, preferably one like southernwood that has rather finely cut leaves. Tie the stems together with a piece of string or knitting wool.

2. Add another circle of a fragrant herb, and tie again. Repeat this process—varying the colors and leaf shapes from row to row and using flowering herbs like mint or marjoram if you have them on hand—until the tussie-mussie is the size you want. Make the last circle with a large-leaved herb such as sage, lamb's ear, or rose geranium.

3. For a formal effect, create a collar for the nosegay by cutting a small hole in the center of a paper doily and slipping it over the stems. Tie the finished tussie-mussie with a ribbon to hold the doily in place.

HERB STANDARDS: TRAINED BEAUTY

Herb standards are plants trained to grow with single stems and lush, geometrically shaped heads. It takes patience and time to turn an herb plant into a standard: you start with a cutting or small plant, then painstakingly pinch and prune and shape for as long as three years. All this effort is rewarded by the result—a perfect scaled-down "tree" with you as its creator. An herb standard, like a hand-stitched quilt or a home-grown meal, is a personal treasure.

Standards are a simple form of topiary, the art of trimming plants and trees into sometimes fantastic shapes. Originated by the Romans, fanciful topiary reached its height during the Renaissance, when every important garden included plants and trees shaped like amazing animals and, sometimes, elaborate tree houses. When eighteenth-century naturalism ended the passion for plants molded by man's imagination, the more exotic topiaries disappeared, leaving only clipped hedges and simple standards behind.

Now interior designers are using small herb standards for their decorative value. Architectural in feeling, they're more visually interesting than many ordinary houseplants and usually more fragrant as well. Planted in formal containers and displayed in pairs, standards appear proper and traditional, but in baskets or clay pots, they look more like escapees from a miniature enchanted forest.

Herb standards can be trained as small as you like—some are just 6 inches high—or as tall as the plant will grow, which is several feet with herbs like bay and rosemary. Large standards are impressive looking indoors as well as out, framing a doorway or edging a terrace.

Paul Leonard's collection of herb standards, far left, is displayed on an antique plant stand. Training herbs like rosemary or lemon geranium around wire hoops, left, is an easy form of topiary. Pat Braun wires flowers on a rosemary topiary for special occasions.

139

Paul Leonard gathers several little standards in a basket for a centerpiece. They could be decorated with flowers for a party, or with tiny pomanders or candies for the holidays. Marston Luce had miniature Versailles boxes made, **above right**, *for his myrtle standards. His formal rosemary standards,* **below right**, *work well with the American country furniture he sells.*

Interior designer Paul Leonard grows his standards on a warm, sunny windowsill in his Connecticut house. Although many people think they need a greenhouse to grow standards, Paul says there's "an advantage to growing them in an unpampered atmosphere. The plants are sturdier and more adaptable when they've matured. A greenhouse plant generally finds it hard to withstand the dry, less hospitable atmosphere of the average house for more than a few days."

Paul believes that growing a standard is like any other creative project: finding what works best for you takes some experimentation. His basic instructions for growing one of these little trees follow. Start here, but, as he says, "if your first try is unsuccessful, don't give up. Simply try again."

How to Grow an Herb Standard

"Growing an herb standard is basically quite easy, but requires a great deal of patience and the strength to be ruthless about pruning," says Paul Leonard. If you start from a cutting, it will be at least a year before you have anything resembling a small tree, and two to three years before you have a good-sized plant, particularly if you're working with slow growers like rosemary, bay, and myrtle.

Here's how Paul grows his little herb "trees."

1. Take a good, straight cutting from a healthy plant, dip the tip in rooting hormone, and plant it in a mixture of equal parts of sand, potting soil, and vermiculite. After watering, you can put a plastic bag over the plant to create a little greenhouse until it begins to form roots, although Paul doesn't bother. In any case,

you must keep the cutting moist or it will wilt. Put it in good light but not where it will get hot sun for long periods.

2. When the cutting shows signs of growth and begins developing new leaves, move it to a spot where it will get plenty of sun. The more light it gets, the thicker the stem will be. To keep the stem straight, turn the plant frequently so it doesn't grow toward the light.

Rather than start with a cutting, you might prefer to buy a small plant from your local herb nursery. Select one with a single, very straight stem, then train it in the same way as the cutting, following the instructions below.

3. Stake the stem to keep it straight as it grows and to give the plant support. Use a stake as tall as you want the mature plant to be; a nonrotting plastic or metal stake is most practical.

142

Attach the plant to it loosely with plastic ties. The stem should have room to grow thicker without being cut by the tie. As the plant grows, add another tie every 3 or 4 inches.

4. Remove all side branches as they form, until the plant has grown to the desired height. Any leaves that appear along the stem should be left to help the plant produce food. Once the stem is as tall as you want it, pinch out the growing tip so that two branches form. At this point you can remove the leaves on the stem and start feeding the plant with an organic fish fertilizer about once a month.

5. When the top branches develop two or three sets of leaves, pinch out their tips, allowing two more sets of branches to form. Keep up this growing and pruning effort until the plant has developed a good crown. As you prune, keep the shape of the finished tree in mind. If the tree needs more width, prune the stem at a leaf bud on its outer side; for greater height, prune where the leaf bud is on the inner side. The crown can be any shape, but the most common is a simple ball.

6. The mature plant will need trimming occasionally, much the way a hedge does, to keep it from getting straggly.

To be trained as a standard an herb must have a straight growing stem, strong enough to support the weight of the head of foliage. The most commonly used herbs are myrtle, rosemary, curry plant, santolina, lemon verbena, sweet bay, scented geranium, roses.

*Paul Leonard, **opposite**, trims one of his herb standards on the herb-dotted patio of his Connecticut home. He roots the cuttings from his "forest" of myrtle trees, **above**, for another crop. To look their best, these small trees, **left**, must be neatly trimmed. The trimming must be done with care, **right**, to maintain the standard's shape.*

143

A little rosemary tree and a tiered display of herbs and fruit are mixed with Christmas greens, old wooden toys, and candles on an antique table in the Lewises' dining room. Herb prints from the 1774 Hortus Romanus *hang above them, with dried leaves tucked behind the frames.*

AN HERBAL CHRISTMAS

To most people, Christmas brings thoughts of pine and fir, juniper, holly, and mistletoe, but to those who love herbs, Christmas is a time when their pleasure in these fragrant greens and colorful flowers can be shared with herbal

*The tiered centerpiece, **above**, of pomanders, fruit, and lavender, purple sage, rosemary, thyme, and artemisias is festooned with streamers of orange peel.*

145

Joy Lewis decorates the small rosemary tree with spice cookies and "snow" made from egg whites and sugar.

Doughboys circle a small rosemary tree in the Lewises' front parlor.

147

*In Nancy Cooley's dining room, the centerpiece, **above**, coordinates with the subtle holiday wreath and mantel decoration, **left**, where gray santolina, sea lavender, catnip, statice, and baby's breath are nestled in sprays of evergreen.*

gifts and aromatic decorations to delight friends and family. Herbs are mixed with evergreens in wreaths and swags; fashioned into old-time kissing balls; shaped into trees and tree decorations; turned into centerpieces for the holiday table; and made into potpourris and pomanders to scent the home or give to friends.

At the Christmas Eve party interior designer Robert K. Lewis and his wife, Joy, host every year, a favorite centerpiece is made by stacking three antique glass cake stands into a tiered display, and topping it with a tall hand-blown glass for more height. Then Bob Lewis makes special pomanders by scoring designs in the peels of oranges and tracing them with lines of cloves. Each

tier of the display is piled with the pomanders mixed with unadorned lemons, oranges, kumquats, and even a small grapefruit. Another pomander sits in the mouth of the glass. Leaves from whatever herbs the garden still has.to offer are tucked among the fruits for additional fragrance and color. (Sprigs of dried herbs could be used if fresh herbs are unavailable.) Finally, graceful strips of orange peel, curling like festive streamers, are draped over the pomander in the glass.

Nancy Cooley, a lecturer on herbs and wreath making, takes a more formal approach to herbal decorations in wreaths and arrangements for the dining room and parlor of her Long Island house, but the family room is decorated with an informal

The arrangement in the parlor, **above left,** *contrasts the simple shapes of magnolia leaves, treated with a glycerine solution to turn them brown, with feathery sprays of rue, artemisia, and juniper. Red apples and pinecones add a holiday feeling. The santolina and boxwood tabletop tree,* **above,** *is decorated with cranberries, crabapples, and uncured olives. A rose-hip wreath,* **right,** *hangs in the kitchen.*

149

At Caprilands, the natural beauty of the fir tree in the barn, **left,** is enhanced with sprigs of silvery artemisia and baby's breath tucked amid the branches and red velvet streamers cascading from the top. Mrs. Simmons attaches Artemisia annua *to a cone-shaped wire frame,* **top,** *to make an everlasting tree. In the greenhouse, the spruce tree,* **above,** *is decorated with dried yarrow, statice, and baby's breath.*

151

tabletop tree of green santolina and boxwood. Even the kitchen
has an herbal wreath: a plump circle of rosy-red dried rose hips.

When Christmas comes to Caprilands, the 300-year-old
Connecticut farm where noted herbalist Adelma Simmons
shares her gardens, cuisine, and knowledge with thousands of
people each year, the house and outbuildings are lavishly
decked with herbs.

In the dining room the beams are thickly hung with
bunches of bittersweet and juniper lush with berries; in another
room balls of pink rosebuds hang overhead. A small crèche
resting on herbs such as lady's bedstraw and thyme, which were
said to have lined the manger, is tucked into a niche by the
dining room fireplace. On a side table, a bowl of Golden Bishop

A Caprilands Christmas classic, Golden Bishop Punch, **top,** *is
garnished with rosemary and set in a living wreath of holly, ivy,
artemisia, pine, rose hips, broom, juniper, cinnamon, nutmegs, bay,
and myrtle. The swag,* **above,** *is made from the harvest of the garden
and nearby fields and woods. Bittersweet and juniper lush with
berries,* **right,** *decorate the dining room ceiling.*

152

Pat Carter welcomes guests to
Muskettoe Pointe Farm, **left**, *with
big baskets of dried herbs and
flowers. She adds the delicate leaf
stalks of fresh salad burnet which
hang gracefully over the edge of
the basket. The Christmas basket,*
above, *is filled with dried herbs, a
tiny herb wreath, cinnamon
sticks, and bayberry candles.*

153

Punch is garnished with rosemary and surrounded by a wreath of fresh herbs.

A tall deep-green fir stands in the barn, festooned with branches of silvery artemisia and baby's breath. In the greenhouse where plants are started and grown during cold weather, a short plump spruce is adorned with bunches of dried yarrow flowers, statice, and baby's breath. Another small tree has been made from dried *Artemisia annua* inserted in a cone-shaped piece of chicken wire.

At the Carter herb farm in Virginia, seen on pages 60–61, Christmas guests are welcomed by a simple, unadorned boxwood wreath made from prunings from the garden, which hangs outside the front door. A huge basket piled high with bunches of beautifully colored dried herbs and flowers sits on one side of the doorstoop. Inside, there's always a traditional family tree in the large open sitting-dining room where the Carters spend much of their time, but this year Pat Carter also decorated another tree to place on a table in the smaller, formal parlor. The little pine, with its sparsely needled limbs and pretty herbal decorations, is not traditional, but its naive charm has a special appeal.

Maria Price, a young herbalist from Maryland, has her own herbal approach to Christmas. She turns a potted bay tree into a small herbal Christmas tree for the family room. In her dining room, Maria has a different kind of herbal tree, actually a tree-shaped arrangement of silver king artemisia and sweet wormwood. A special wreath of flowers and herbs she grows and dries hangs proudly over the living room mantel, an exquisite testimony to Maria's sense of color and design, and to the possibilities for holiday beauty in herbs.

Even salamis become a festive holiday gift, **right,** *when they're decorated with lavender and cinnamon. The small Christmas tree in the Carters' front parlor,* **far right,** *is hung with nosegays of globe amaranth, yarrow, statice, and lavender,* **opposite,** *as well as tiny red hearts for extra color.*

154

Maria Price's miniature Christmas tree is actually a tree-shaped arrangement of silver king artemisia and sweet wormwood with celosia, santolina buds, feverfew, and garlic chive blossoms to add texture and color. Tiny pomander birds and angels made from a mixture of herbs and spices hang from the branches.

156

Frosted gingerbread men and little tussie-mussies made of "any herbs or dried flowers you find pleasing," **left**, *turn Maria's potted bay tree,* **above**, *into a Christmas tree.*

157

The spectacular Christmas wreath that hangs over the Prices' fireplace contains roses, globe amaranth, strawflowers, celosia, lavender, bits of statice, santolina buds and leaves, artemisias, and scented geranium leaves.

HERBS IN THE KITCHEN

*H*erbs bring out the best in foods, enhancing the flavor and sensory appeal of almost every dish. If you need to be convinced, just think of plain tomatoes, bread, lamb, fish; then think of juicy red tomatoes sprinkled with fresh basil, a just-baked loaf redolent of dill and parsley, a roast leg of lamb seasoned with garlic and rosemary, a grilled sea bass flavored with fennel. And there's a world of possibilities beyond familiar herbs such as parsley, chives, and dill.

Herbs can make a familiar dish new or lift an ordinary entrée to

Everything from vinegar to cookies, **left,** *is enhanced by the special flavor of herbs. Garlic,* **above left,** *and chili peppers,* **above right,** *dry in the sun.*

161

gourmet status. They can perform the same subtle magic with soups, stews, salads, breads, and even desserts. And with a bouquet of herbs or a scattering of herb flowers used as garnish, your food will look as wonderful as it tastes.

The best way to learn about cooking with herbs is to try out recipes that call for only a single herb, so you become familiar with its characteristics and the foods it enhances. Then begin mixing the herb with others. Just remember that it's best to avoid combining two strong herbs such as sage and rosemary. And when you use a strong and a delicate herb in the same dish, keep the most aromatic herb to a minimum so the more delicate one doesn't become overpowered. You have only to add too much of an herb to know how devastating the effect can be.

Experiment with edible flowers, too. They're as tasty as they are pretty.

At Chez Panisse, Alice Waters serves fresh blackberries in a pool of subtly rose-flavored crème anglaise. *The final touch is a scattering of petals from a fresh rose.*

Maria Price decorates "peach" cookies with a sugared mint leaf. (The recipe is on page 224.)

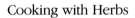

Cooking with Herbs

Fresh herbs can be substituted for dry herbs in most recipes, although it often doesn't work as well in reverse. You must remember that fresh herbs are not as strong as their dried counterparts so you'll have to adjust amounts. The basic rule is 1 tablespoon of fresh herbs for each teaspoon of dried herbs, or 3 to 1.

Because fresh herbs lose their flavor when cooked for any length of time, they taste best added to the pot a few minutes

before the dish is done, or sprinkled over food before it's served. One exception to this is bay, which releases its flavor only during long cooking.

Preserving Herbs for Cooking

The most aromatic herbs, like thyme, rosemary, winter savory, sage, and bay, seem to dry with almost as much flavor as they have when fresh. Only a few herbs, like parsley, chives, and basil, retain so little of their fresh flavor after drying that it's not

worth trying to preserve them this way. Others, although they lose some of their zest in drying, still deserve space on your kitchen shelf. And even if they're a bit less aromatic when dried, you'll be amazed at how much more flavorful they'll be than those ground herbs found in most supermarkets and groceries. Directions for drying herbs are offered on pages 106–7.

Dried herbs tend to lose their pungency when exposed to light and heat, so store them in a dim, cool place in tightly stoppered jars. Avoid keeping them near the stove, even though it's handy. The flavor of properly stored herbs will begin to dissipate after about six months; after a year you should replace them. Luckily, by that time your garden will be ready with another fragrant crop.

Freezing is an alternative to drying, and most herbs retain a great deal of flavor this way. Frozen herbs can be used in the same quantities as fresh herbs for cooking, but because the herbs become limp and sometimes discolored in the process, they are not very appetizing in salads or as garnishes. Small bunches of herbs like mint and chives can be well wrapped in foil, then stored in the freezer; the herbs may be cut off and chopped as needed. Or you can prechop the herbs, pack them in a plastic container, and spoon out the amount required. Whole basil leaves may be frozen in a container, too, then taken out individually. Although they may turn black, the flavor of the basil leaves is almost as strong as if they were just picked from the garden. If you like fresh mint sauce, chop mint leaves and pack them with sugar in the quantities your recipe requires and freeze. When you're ready for the sauce, put some of the sugared mint in a pan, add vinegar, and heat to the boiling point.

Another simple method of preserving herbs that works particularly well with coriander and dill weed is puréeing the fresh leaves with a little water and freezing the purée in ice trays. Once the herbs are frozen, store them in a bag in the freezer, and add a cube to soups, stews, or sauces as they cook. One cube will equal about 1 tablespoon of fresh herb. Basil can also be preserved this way, or puréed with oil for storing in the freezer or the refrigerator. The basil is then ready to be turned into *pesto* or to add its flavor to soups and sauces.

Freshly picked herbs and cheery calendula, the poor man's saffron, **opposite top left,** *are for sale on a Nantucket street corner. Herbs added to canned tomatoes, pickles, and other foods,* **opposite bottom left,** *give them extra flavor. When Pat Carter serves lunch,* **opposite,** *at her Virginia farmhouse, fresh herbs season the food and decorate the platters* *and the table. Dill and thyme garnish the salads, pineapple sage spikes the iced tea, and yarrow, foxglove, and deep-purple sage flowers make a charming country bouquet. A rose geranium leaf imparts a subtle flavor to apple jelly,* **above left.** *Onions, garlic, and shallots,* **left,** *await the cook in a French country market.*

165

HERBAL BEGINNINGS

Many herbs have a reputation as appetite stimulants, so what better way to start a meal than with a dish temptingly flavored with one of them? You might try an accent of bittersweet dill, fiery chili pepper, savory caraway, spicy cumin, or pungent fennel. Mint, basil, rosemary, sorrel, sage, and ginger are a few of the other herbs that can be incorporated into many of your favorite recipes.

Add sage to savory cheese crisps to pass around with cocktails; sprinkle ginger over melon to serve as an appetizer; spread thin toast triangles with basil-flavored *pesto* to accompany soup. Or scatter a few leaves of chopped basil or mint on a homemade chicken broth; some chopped nasturtium leaves and flowers on potato soup? And what could be a nicer start to a summer dinner than the basil-flavored tomato sorbet on page 171?

Here are a few more delectable recipes that will show you the herbal possibilities for appetizers and first courses.

SAGE FRITTERS

Serves 6

Sage fritters were first made by the Romans thousands of years ago, and luckily for us, the art has been passed down to their modern ancestors. Although traditionally eaten after dinner to aid digestion, these tender little fritters are a wonderful accompaniment to drinks or a soup course, too. Sage fritters are the most pungent and stimulating to the appetite, but borage with its slight cucumber flavor, basil, or sorrel also make interesting fritters.

  3 dozen fresh sage leaves
  1 tablespoon butter
  ½ cup all-purpose flour
    Pinch of salt
  ¼ cup milk
    Vegetable oil, for frying
  1 extra-large egg white

Carefully wash and dry the sage leaves, to avoid bruising. In a saucepan, melt the butter in ½ cup water over low heat. Set aside to cool to lukewarm.

Combine the flour and salt in a bowl. Gradually blend in the butter-water mixture and the milk, beating until the batter is smooth. Cover and let stand at room temperature for 1 hour.

Preheat the oven to 300°. Heat about 1 inch of oil in a large skillet. The temperature is right when a little drop of the dough browns quickly but doesn't burn. In a bowl, beat the egg white until stiff but not dry. Gently fold the white into the batter. Dip a few of the sage leaves in the batter and drop them one at a time into the oil to cook. Do not overcrowd the pan. Fry until the fritters are golden brown on both sides, turning once during cooking.

Using a slotted spoon, remove the fritters from the oil and drain on paper towels. Keep warm in the oven until all of the fritters are cooked, then serve at once.

167

STUFFED CLAMS

Serves 6

Chris Mead, whose garden is shown on pages 34–35, takes clams fresh from the bay near his house, chops them, adds herbs, and then scoops them back into their shells before broiling. He serves the clams as an appetizer for dinner or the main dish for a summer lunch.

  3 dozen cherrystone clams
  3 celery ribs
  1 onion
  3 cups dried bread crumbs
  4 tablespoons butter, melted
     Finely grated zest of 2 lemons
     Juice of 1 lemon
  2 teaspoons dried thyme or 2 tablespoons chopped fresh
  3 teaspoons dried oregano or 3 tablespoons chopped fresh
     Salt and freshly ground pepper

Clean the clams. Remove them from the shells, reserving 24 small halves for serving. Coarsely chop the clams, celery, and onion. (If you use a food processor, be sure not to overprocess.)

Melt the butter in a large saucepan. Add the clams, celery, onion, bread crumbs, and ½ cup water to the melted butter and mix well. Stir in half of the lemon zest (reserving the other half for garnish) and all of the lemon juice and fresh herbs. Season with salt and pepper and mix well.

Preheat the broiler. Divide the clam mixture among the 24 clam shells. Arrange the shells on a baking sheet and place under the broiler for about 10 minutes, or until browned on top. Garnish with lemon zest and serve.

HERBED WALNUTS

Makes 1 pound roasted nuts

Rosemary-flavored walnuts are a delicious accompaniment to pre-dinner drinks. The herb makes the nuts more interesting than the usual coating of salt. For variety, try this recipe with sage; or roast cashews with powdered cumin or almonds with ground ginger. Roasting nuts in the oven is simple, and you'll find the results far superior to the preroasted nuts you can buy.

2 tablespoons butter
2 tablespoons olive oil
1 pound walnut halves
1½ tablespoons crushed dried rosemary or 5 tablespoons finely chopped fresh
1 teaspoon paprika
2 teaspoons salt

Preheat the oven to 325°. Place the butter and the oil in a large pan and melt in the oven. Scatter the nuts in the pan, stir them to coat with the butter-oil mixture,

then spread them out in a single layer.

Scatter the rosemary, paprika, and salt evenly over the nuts. Bake for 20 to 25 minutes, shaking and stirring several times until the nuts are golden brown but not burned. Drain, if necessary, on paper towels and serve warm or at room temperature.

Herb-flavored stuffed clams, **opposite,** *are served in an antique berry basket. A garland of fresh rosemary circles herb-roasted nuts,* **above.**

REFRESHING HERBAL SORBETS

At the turn of the century, a sorbet was always served to cleanse and refresh the palate between the courses of a fine meal. "Americans appreciate food more now than they have any time since then," says Peter Godoff. "But it's a different kind of food," he adds. "Nouvelle cuisine has focused interest on lighter food, small portions, and fresh ingredients." Fresh fruit sorbets are part of the nouvelle cuisine repertoire, and Peter thinks health-conscious America is ready for a sorbet revival. That's why he started American Glacé, a company that makes sorbets with fresh fruits and herbs, no cholesterol, and fewer calories than in frozen yogurt.

The new cuisine—"a cuisine of spontaneity that takes what's fresh that day and cooks it quickly," as he defines it, reinforced Peter's interest in herbs.

When he started experimenting with sorbets, he liked the idea of including herbs in both dessert and first- or between-course versions. Using herbs from his terrace garden as well as from his well-stocked neighborhood greengrocer, Peter spent hours with his home-sized ice-cream machine working out recipes that he now produces professionally. His sorbets, he says, are an excellent way for people to experience the flavor of an herb they may have been using but never really tasting.

All the sorbet recipes here have the same base: a "tea" made by cooking the herb in a simple syrup, the sugar-and-water mixture that is the fundamental ingredient of all sorbets. These teas keep well in the freezer, so you can make large batches in the summer when herbs are plentiful and then in December and January savor the fresh herb taste.

Sorbets made in an ice-cream machine have a smoother texture than those frozen in the freezer of your refrigerator. Peter thinks sorbets are at their peak fresh from the machine, their consistency just short of firm; but you can, of course, store these machine-made sorbets in the freezer. The consistency will become slightly grainy, but the flavor will not be harmed.

If you don't have an ice-cream machine, you can freeze sorbets in ice trays. When they're half frozen, take them out, stir well, then return the trays to the freezer until the sorbets are firm. Sorbets made by this method will be grainy: you may have to break them up with a fork or, for a smooth consistency closer to that you get with a machine, put them in a food processor for just a minute before serving.

The following recipes were created by Peter specifically for small ice-cream machines or the home freezer.

BASIC HERB SYRUP ("TEA") FOR SORBETS

2 cups sugar
¼ cup whichever chopped fresh herb is specified in recipe
5 cups water

Place the sugar, herbs, and water in a saucepan. Bring to a boil, stirring occasionally to dissolve the sugar. When the syrup reaches the boiling point, reduce the heat to low and simmer for 5 minutes. Let the "tea" cool to room temperature, then refrigerate overnight. In the morning, strain the syrup and discard the herb.

All the recipes that follow make 1 quart of sorbet. For dessert sorbets, see page 226.

Cooling rosemary sorbet, **opposite,** *can be decorated with frosted rosemary made by dipping a sprig in lightly beaten egg white, then in sugar. A bright-green basil leaf enhances delicate pink tomato basil sorbet,* **below.**

TOMATO AND BASIL SORBET

Makes 1 quart

1¼ cups basil syrup, made according to the preceding basic instructions.
2½ cups fresh tomato purée
1 tablespoon tomato paste
¼ cup Russian red pepper vodka*
1 teaspoon fresh lemon juice

Combine all of the ingredients in a bowl and freeze in an ice-cream machine or in the freezing compartment of your refrigerator. If you use the freezer, stir the frozen sorbet to break up the ice crystals and refreeze. Stir again, if desired, refreezing each time, to produce a smoother sorbet.

*If red pepper vodka is not available, use ¼ cup of vodka in which you have steeped ¼ teaspoon of cayenne pepper for 24 hours.

ROSEMARY SORBET

Makes 1 quart

¼ cup rosemary
2 cups sugar
5 cups water
2 cups dry white wine
6 tablespoons fresh lemon juice

Add the rosemary to the sugar and water in a saucepan and prepare rosemary syrup according to the basic instructions.

In a bowl, blend 2½ cups of the syrup with the wine and lemon juice. Freeze in an ice-cream machine or in the freezing compartment of your refrigerator. If you are using the freezer, stir the frozen sorbet to break up the ice crystals and refreeze. Stir again, if desired, refreezing each time, to produce a smoother sorbet.

BAKING WITH HERBS

Perhaps coming from a family of bakers has made me more susceptible than most to the tantalizing aromas of breads and cakes, cookies and pies, baking in the oven. When these aromas are enhanced by the addition of herbs, they are for me as close to perfection as scents can be.

Any bread, muffin, scone, biscuit, or tea bread is a candidate for the touch of herbs. Try the recipes here, then gather your favorite herbs from the garden and experiment with others.

IRISH SCONES

Makes 32 scones

These scones, inspired by Irish soda bread, contrast the warm, spicy taste of caraway seeds with the sweetness of currants.

2	sticks plus 2 tablespoons butter
5½	cups all-purpose flour
¾	cup sugar
¼	cup baking powder
1½	cups sour milk (you can sour sweet milk by adding a few drops of lemon juice and letting it stand a few minutes)
½	cup yogurt
2½	tablespoons caraway seeds
1¼	cups currants
1	large egg yolk, beaten

Preheat the oven to 350°. Cut the butter into little pieces and put in a bowl. Add the flour, sugar, and baking powder. Using a pastry blender (or two knives), cut the butter into the dry ingredients until they have the texture of coarse cornmeal.

Mix the sour milk and yogurt together and add to the flour mixture, stirring it in quickly but gently with a fork. Turn the slightly sticky dough out onto a floured board, pour the caraway seeds and currants on top, and quickly knead them in, working the dough as little as possible.

Divide the dough into 4 equal parts. Pat each part into a circle 1 inch thick, then cut each circle into 8 pie-shaped pieces. Put the pieces on a lightly floured baking sheet and brush the tops with the beaten egg yolk. Bake approximately 15 minutes or until golden brown and cooked through.

Ordinary scones become special with the addition of caraway seeds and currants, **right***. A puffy golden-brown herbed* gougère, **opposite**, *can be served with drinks or as a first course.*

172

HERBED GOUGÈRE

Serves 6

Gougère, *a puffy, cheese-flavored pastry, is a traditional French cocktail accompaniment. Adding the aromatic leaves of dill, parsley, and chives is a tasty variation on the basic recipe. Bake the dough as individual puffs for hors d'oeuvres or shape it into a big ring for an appetizer. Filling the center of the ring with chicken, fish, or shrimp salad makes it a lovely dish for a summer lunch.*

- 8 tablespoons (1 stick) butter
- ¼ teaspoon salt
- 1 cup all-purpose flour
- 4 eggs
- 1 cup coarsely grated Gruyère cheese
- 1 tablespoon chopped fresh parsley
- 1 tablespoon chopped fresh dill
- 1 tablespoon chopped fresh chives

In a saucepan, combine the butter, salt, and 1 cup water. Bring to a boil. Off the heat, add the flour all at once and beat well with a wooden spoon until the flour is incorporated. Return the saucepan to moderate heat and cook until the dough becomes quite stiff and pulls away from the sides of the pan.

Remove from the heat and beat in the eggs, one at a time. Stir in ⅔ cup of the cheese and all the chopped herbs.

Preheat the oven to 425°. Drop the dough by tablespoonfuls onto an ungreased baking sheet to make individual puffs, or drop the dough by tablespoonfuls to form a ring. Sprinkle with remaining cheese. Bake for 25 to 30 minutes, or until puffed and golden brown. Serve warm.

173

PESTO BREAD

Makes 2 loaves

This pesto-laden loaf is delicious with simple grilled meats and makes a perfect accompaniment for cheese and tomatoes at a picnic or a light supper of soup and salad. An easy French-type loaf, the bread is based on a recipe I learned in a James Beard cooking class long ago.

Pesto (recipe follows)
1½ packages active dry yeast
2 cups warm water (105° to 115°)
1½ teaspoons salt

1 tablespoon sugar
6 to 7 cups all-purpose flour
Yellow or white cornmeal, for the baking sheet

Make the *pesto.* In a large bowl, dissolve the yeast in the warm water and add the salt and sugar. Stir thoroughly. Set aside briefly until foamy.

Using a wooden spoon, beat in the flour, one cup at a time, until a smooth dough forms. Turn out on a lightly floured board and let rest a few minutes, then knead until the dough is elastic. Place in a lightly oiled bowl, cover with a towel, and set in a warm, draft-free place until doubled in volume, about 1½ hours.

Turn the dough out onto a lightly floured board, punch it down, and knead again. Divide the dough in half. Pat out 2 rectangles, each about 10 by 12 inches, and spread a thin layer of the *pesto* mixture over each, leaving a 1-inch border. Starting with a long side, roll each rectangle of the dough into a cylinder and shape into a loaf. Allow the loaves to rise for 5 minutes.

Sprinkle a baking sheet with cornmeal and place the loaves on it. Brush each loaf with cold water and place in a cold oven. Place a pan of boiling water in the bottom of the oven and turn the oven to 400°. Bake the bread for 35 to 40 minutes, or until the loaves are browned and sound hollow when rapped on the bottom. Place the bread on a rack to cool slightly and serve warm for the greatest flavor.

PESTO

2 cups fresh basil leaves
½ cup parsley leaves
½ cup olive oil
2 garlic cloves
1 teaspoon salt
½ cup freshly grated Parmesan cheese

Purée the basil, parsley, oil, garlic, and salt in a blender or processor. Stir in the cheese. Store any leftover *pesto* in the refrigerator with a thin layer of oil on top, or freeze.

Pungent basil pesto *is swirled through this crusty loaf,* **above left.** *For variety, try the recipe with other herbs like coriander, parsley, or dill.*

174

Decorated with flowering lemon thyme and lemon balm, double lemon tea bread looks as good as it tastes.

LEMON TEA BREAD

Makes 1 loaf

Lemony herbs and lemon juice give this bread its flavor.

¾	cup milk
1	tablespoon finely chopped lemon balm
1	tablespoon finely chopped lemon thyme
2	cups all-purpose flour
1½	teaspoons baking powder
¼	teaspoon salt
6	tablespoons butter, at room temperature
1	cup sugar
2	eggs
1	tablespoon grated lemon zest

Butter a 9 by 5 by 3-inch pan. Preheat the oven to 325°. Heat the milk with the chopped herbs and let steep until cool.

Mix the flour, baking powder, and salt together in a bowl. In another bowl, cream the butter and gradually beat in the sugar. Continue beating until light and fluffy. Beat in the eggs, one at a time. Beat in the lemon zest. Add the flour mixture alternately with the herbed milk. Mix until the batter is just blended.

Put the batter into the prepared pan. Bake for about 50 minutes, or until a toothpick inserted in the center comes out dry. Remove from the pan onto a wire rack that is set over a sheet of waxed paper. Pour Lemon Glaze over the still-hot bread. Decorate with a few sprigs of lemon thyme.

LEMON GLAZE

Juice of 2 lemons
Confectioners' sugar

Put the lemon juice in a bowl and add the sugar, stirring until a thick but still pourable paste forms. Pour the glaze over the hot bread.

All the cheeses on this tray were made from the same simple cream cheese recipe. The variety is provided by the different herbs and the range of shapes.

CHEESES MADE FOR HERBS

The Marquis de Montferrier and his wife live in a beautiful old house that was once the residence of the principal farmer of the Château de Villandry. It was here that tenant farmers brought produce from their fields as their rent. The lovely old antique-filled house opens onto a terrace overlooking a garden and a little pond—a surprisingly elegant setting for a goat farm and *fromagerie.* The large barn on one side of the house holds a herd of pure-white pedigreed goats bred primarily for the milk the Marquise turns into delicious goat cheese.

After apprenticing for the three years required by French law, the Marquise is now a licensed producer of farm-made goat cheese. In her small white *fromagerie,* she combines the milk from the morning and evening milkings, adds rennet, and leaves the mixture to form a curd which will be put into cheese molds to drain. Cheese from previous milkings sits draining and drying on trays in front of the blue-trimmed window.

The cheeses are traditionally shaped: the flat-topped pyramid called Valencay, flat-topped cones of Selles, long logs of Sainte Maures, and small disks known as Crottins. Some are flavored with a pungent coating of dried basil and savory or with pepper; others are covered with a thin film of vegetable ash to help preserve moisture. After they've dried adequately in the *fromagerie,* the cheeses to be used fresh—mild flavored, soft, and moist in texture—are delivered to local restaurants or sold at nearby open-air markets. The remaining cheeses are removed to a specially refrigerated area to ripen. During the aging process, the taste becomes sharper, the texture drier and firmer. The cheeses can be eaten at various stages of aging, depending on personal preference.

English cheesemaker John Saunders makes herbed goat cheese, **above,** *in traditional French heart molds.*

177

Fresh goat cheeses from the Calistro Dairy in England, **opposite,** *are marinated in herb-flavored oil for extra taste. The door leads to the de Montferrier's fromagerie,* **top,** *where herbed goat cheeses dry on a tray in front of the window,* **left.** *The purebred goats,* **above,** *gather in the barnyard.*

179

Cheesemaking on a small scale is springing up in England and the United States, too. When John Sanders and his wife, Sandy, found themselves flooded with extra milk from the Angora goats they were breeding at their farm south of London, they headed for France to find out how to make cheese. After observing French goat-cheese makers, they bought some traditional molds in the shape of hearts, logs, and bells and returned to their goat herd in England. Now they make 100 cheeses a day, flavoring some with chives and peppers, soaking others in herb-flavored olive oil, leaving still others plain. They sell all they can produce to local cheese shops, restaurants, and people who buy cheese at the farm.

Gail LeCompte started America's first (and now largest) commercial goat-cheese operation at her New Jersey farm in 1979. She had learned cheesemaking by experimenting in her kitchen, aided by tips from her chemist husband and a professor of dairy science at Rutgers University. Gail produces traditional French-style cheeses—fresh Chèvre mixed with a blend of herbs, small fresh Crottins rolled in herbs, as well as plain cheeses, and Saanen, a nontraditional semisoft slicing cheese she developed. Pieces of Saanen are sometimes soaked in olive oil that has been flavored with oregano and a touch of thyme and garlic.

Gail advises anyone making cheese at home to be sure and pasturize the milk by bringing it to 145 degrees and holding it at that temperature for 30 minutes. "This produces a healthier, better-lasting product," she says. If you buy goat's milk, check it as most likely it will be pasturized already. Beginners at cheesemaking would benefit from reading Garden Way's *Cheesemaking Made Easy,* she advises. The book was written by Ricki and Bob Carroll, a young New England couple who have turned an interest in cheesemaking into a prosperous mail-order business.

Simple fresh cheeses can be flavored with herbs and spices in many different ways. Try the recipes here. When you see how easy they are, you may want to buy a book on the subject (see the Directory page 241) and go on to make the slightly more complicated hard cheeses, or the soft, runny types like Brie.

180

A SIMPLE FRESH CHEESE

Makes 1½ to 2 cups cheese

There are only two steps to creating a simple fresh cheese: making the curd and draining it. Aging is not necessary. Rennet is generally added to the milk to hasten the curding process, but even without rennet a curd will eventually form. Warm weather speeds up the process, but if you're using rennet, don't be impatient and try to rush the curding by adding more. The cheese will have a better flavor if you let it take a little more time to develop.

- 1 quart goat's milk (or cow's milk if goat's milk is not available)
- 2 cups heavy cream
- 3 tablespoons buttermilk
- 1 rennet tablet or ⅛ teaspoon liquid rennet
- 1 teaspoon salt

Heat the milk, cream, and buttermilk to 100°; do not overheat. Stir in the rennet and let stand until the curd is solid and has separated from the whey. Drain off the whey and discard or remove it for another use. Cut the curd into 1-inch squares and place the curds into a cheese mold or a sieve lined with a double layer of dampened cheesecloth. Place the mold on a rack over a bowl and let the cheese drain.

When the cheese has thoroughly drained, unmold it and work in the salt. Reshape, wrap in plastic, and store in the refrigerator until ready to use.

VARIATIONS

Herbed Cheese: Roll the finished cheese in a mixture of dried, crushed savory, rosemary, thyme, and marjoram.

Savory Cheese Squares: Cut the finished cheese into small squares or form it into small balls and roll some in paprika, some in fennel seed, some in dried savory, and some in curry powder. Serve with drinks.

Spicy Dessert Cheese: Add ¼ teaspoon salt, ½ teaspoon pepper, 1 teaspoon ground ginger, and 2 whole cloves to the curd when you put it in the mold.

Garlic Herb Cheese: Add a peeled garlic clove to the warm milk; remove when curd has formed. Add ½ teaspoon chopped fresh chives, 1 teaspoon chopped fresh parsley, ½ teaspoon chopped fresh savory, ½ teaspoon chopped fresh thyme, and 1 teaspoon chopped fresh marjoram to the curd when you put it in the mold or work in with the salt.

Cheese in Herbed Oil: Put 2 cups olive oil, 1 garlic clove, 1 sprig fresh thyme, 1 sprig fresh rosemary, 1 bay leaf, 1 red chili pepper, 6 peppercorns, 6 coriander seeds, and 2 whole allspice in a wide-mouthed jar with a lid. Add 3 or 4 small fresh cheeses. They will keep at room temperature and can be replaced with new cheeses as they are used.

Savory Cheese: Wrap one or two sprigs of fresh savory around the cheese and let it absorb the flavor for several days.

French farm cheeses in different stages of drying, **opposite,** *are seasoned with sprigs of savory laid on top. These types of cheese are often sold at small roadside stands,* **right,** *in the French countryside.*

A collection of herb vinegars, **opposite,** *sits on the windowsill at Hullbrook House Herbs. Herb vinegars are appealing to the eye,* **left,** *as well as the taste.*

HERBED VINEGARS AND OILS

Bottles of fine vinegars or pure oils filled with sprigs of herbs and spices allow you to enjoy the taste of fresh herbs year round. Flavored oils and vinegars give a special tang to salads, sauces, stews, marinades, and grilled and sautéed dishes. Old-time farmers even added a spoonful of vinegar laced with an herb like mint to an ice-filled glass of plain soda to create a wonderfully refreshing drink on a hot day.

Many herbs make good vinegars. Tarragon vinegar is probably the best known, but there's also burnet and borage, with their mild cucumber flavor (adding borage flowers to white vinegar will tint it a lovely pale blue); dill, prettiest when whole seed heads and a few leaves float in the bottle; mint for lamb dishes and fruit salads; lemon thyme for fish; basil for tomatoes; sage for marinating rich meats and fowl; faintly oniony chive blossoms; and even the buds, flowers, and leaves of peppery nasturtiums.

Two or more herbs can be combined and seeds, spices, garlic, or lemon added—just decide which flavor you want to dominate and adjust the amounts of each herb according to its strength. Dill vinegar is particularly delicious when a little lemon and garlic are added to the bottle; combinations of basil, borage, and burnet, or tarragon, lemon thyme, basil, chive blossoms, and burnet work well in salads.

In the English countryside south of London, Elaine Fried has developed a business, Hullbrook House Herbs, based on inventive herbed vinegars and oils. Local ladies help grow most of the herbs for this cottage industry, and then bottle them, with the aid of a small machine, to send to stores all over England.

183

When Elaine faces a shortage of a particular herb, she appeals to the nation's gardeners. Once she knocked at every door in her village to see if anyone had rosemary to spare. She finally enlisted the aid of the Herb Society, whose members throughout England sent her rosemary at twopence a sprig. All Hullbrook House products are based on cider vinegar, which Elaine finds less acidic and a better complement to herbs than wine vinegar.

Elaine has now added herbed oils to her line. Less common than vinegars, they are just as useful for giving instant seasoning to foods. Elaine's highly spiced Oriental wok oil provides stir-fried foods with a Chinese flavor. Another oil, scented with wild Mediterranean herbs like thyme and rosemary, makes a quick pasta sauce. A robust barbeque oil, with garlic, chili, rosemary, and other herbs, serves as a

marinade and basting sauce for grilled meats. And an oil with peppermint, garlic, cumin, coriander, galingale, fennugreek, cloves, mace, and fennel adds a taste of the Middle East.

How to Make Herbed Vinegar

You can use the leaves, seeds, and flowers, singly or in combination, of freshly picked herbs to make herbed vinegars. The vinegar should be the best of the cider or wine varieties available, as herbs will not disguise the sharpness of a bad vinegar.

1. Pick the herbs for the vinegar in the morning after the dew has dried but before the heat of day has driven off some of the essential oils that give herbs their flavor. Use only perfect leaves and flowers, discarding any that have turned brown or show signs of having been eaten by garden pests.

2. Bruise the herbs slightly before putting them in a glass bottle or ceramic crock with a tightly fitting top. Use about ½ cup of herbs for each pint of vinegar, more if you want a stronger taste.

3. Then follow one of the two traditional methods:

1. Pour the vinegar over the herbs in a clear glass bottle and close tightly. Set the bottle in a sunny window for two weeks, turning it frequently.

2. Heat the vinegar; then pour the hot vinegar over the herbs in a bottle or crock and close tightly. Let steep overnight.

3. Whichever method you use, you may want to strain and rebottle the vinegar at the end of the steeping time, adding a fresh, unbruised sprig for decoration. This is a matter of aesthetics—a choice between one simple sprig in the bottle or the generous bunch of herbs used to flavor the vinegar.

How to Make Herbed Oils

Herbed oils can be as simple or as complex as you like. To make your own, simply add the desired herbs and spices to the oil (olive oil is best, but you can also use a good vegetable oil) and steep in a closed bottle or container in a warm but not hot place for a few weeks before using.

Beverly Jacomini uses bottles of herb vinegar, **opposite,** *as a centerpiece for a casual luncheon at her Texas farmhouse. Large jugs of herb vinegar,* **left,** *brew in the sun before being strained and rebottled. Sandy Greig makes chive vinegar by setting the jars on a bench in her garden,* **above,** *so the sun can extract the gentle onion flavor and rosy color of the chive blossoms. A single herb or a compatible mixture,* **below left,** *such as basil, oregano in blossom, thyme, and parsley, can be used to flavor vinegar. Window shelves are filled with a colorful selection of herb vinegars, sweet herb syrups, and teas,* **below right.**

HERBED MAIN COURSES

Americans have traditionally used herbs such as thyme, parsley, and rosemary to season main-course dishes. But recently foreign foods and *nouvelle cuisine* have become almost as familiar as roast lamb, introducing us to once-ignored herbs like cumin and coriander and giving us the freedom to experiment with new tastes and ingredients.

A PIZZA OVEN FULL OF HERBS

Carolyn Dille and Susan Belsinger met, appropriately enough, at a pizza oven in an old country house in Italy, where they both were guests at a weekend party. They discovered their mutual love of cooking when it turned out that they were the only ones willing to stay in the kitchen to stoke the oven's fire. Twelve years later, they're still cooking together: as owners of a successful catering business in the Washington-Baltimore area, coauthors of *Cooking with Herbs,* and teachers of classes on cooking and herbs.

And now they have their own pizza oven, a slightly smaller version of the one that brought them together in Italy, specially designed for the new house Susan and her husband built. The choice of wood and the quality of the fire are almost as important as the recipes in cooking pizzas in the brick oven. In Italy, oak and birch are commonly used as fuel: Susan burns these as well as cherry. "You actually get a different taste from different woods," says Carolyn, "and as unbelievable as it may seem, the crust is a different color." It takes time for the oven to heat to the proper temperature, and it takes experience to know exactly when the fire is hot enough and the bricks have stored enough heat to keep up the oven temperature while the pizza cooks.

You don't need a special oven to cook wonderful pizzas, though; you can use a regular oven and bake pies on a kiln shelf from a local pottery store, as Carolyn does. Kiln shelves are simply clay slabs that act as baking sheets. "They're basically the same as the commercial pizza bricks sold in gourmet shops, but are much cheaper and work as well or better," Susan advises. "Pizzas can be baked on a regular metal baking sheet, of course, but the crust won't be as close to the wonderfully crisp ones that the brick oven or kiln shelf produce."

*The pizza con pancetta, is sprinkled with fresh herbs after being pulled from the oven. The greenhouse off Susan's kitchen, **right**, provides Susan and Carolyn with herbs all winter long.*

PIZZA CON PANCETTA

Serves 3 or 4 as an appetizer

PIZZA DOUGH

Makes two 9–10-inch pizzas

- 1 tablespoon (1 package) active dry yeast
  Pinch of sugar
- ¼ cup warm water (105° to 115°)
- 2 cups unbleached all-purpose white flour
- ¼ cup whole-wheat flour
- ⅔ cup warm water
- 1 tablespoon olive oil
- ½ teaspoon salt

In a small bowl, dissolve the yeast and sugar in ¼ cup warm water. Set aside until foamy. In a large bowl, combine the flours and make a well in the center. When the yeast is foamy, add it to the well. Mix lightly with the surrounding flour and let the sponge rise for about 10 minutes.

Gradually add ⅔ cup warm water, working in the flour as you go. About halfway through this step, stir in the olive oil and salt. Incorporate as much flour as the sponge will take and still remain a bit sticky, though very lively.

Knead the dough lightly for 10 minutes. Let the dough rise until doubled in bulk, 45 minutes to 1½ hours. Punch the dough down and let it rest for 15 minutes before forming into pizza rounds.

187

PIZZA TOPPING

- 6 ounces *pancetta* or salt pork
- 6 ounces whole-milk mozzarella cheese
- 2 pounds firm ripe tomatoes or 1 can (28 ounces) plum tomatoes
- 3 or 4 garlic cloves
- 5 or 6 fresh sage sprigs
- 5 or 6 Italian parsley sprigs
- 1 small onion
- 2 to 3 tablespoons olive oil
   Salt and freshly ground pepper
   Freshly grated Parmesan cheese, for garnish

Unroll the *pancetta* and cut it into ¼-inch dice. In a heavy skillet, render the *pancetta* over low heat for about 15 minutes, until golden brown. Remove with a slotted spoon and set aside.

Grate the mozzarella and set aside.

Peel, seed, and dice the fresh tomatoes or drain and dice the canned tomatoes. Peel and mince the garlic. Stem and chop the sage and parsley medium-fine. Cut the onion in half lengthwise and slice each half into thin rings.

Place a baker's tile on the bottom oven shelf and preheat the oven to 500° for 15 minutes.

Divide the pizza dough into two equal parts. Wrap and refrigerate half of the dough. On a lightly floured pizza paddle, form the remaining piece of dough into a 9- or 10-inch round. Brush the dough lightly with olive oil. Sprinkle half of the garlic and one-third of the herbs on the pizza. Scatter half the *pancetta* over the herbs. Arrange half of the onion rings over the

pancetta. Cover with half of the diced tomatoes and season lightly with salt and pepper.

Slide the pizza onto the baker's tile and bake for 3 to 4 minutes.

Slide the pizza out of the oven; cover with half the mozzarella. Bake the pizza for 3 to 4 minutes more, until the crust is puffed around the edges and light golden brown. The cheese should bubble and just begin to color.

Remove the pizza to a cutting board and sprinkle it with the remaining chopped herbs. Cut into 8 pieces and serve immediately with Parmesan cheese as garnish. Make the other pizza in the same manner.

Experimenting with different combinations of ingredients, **top,** *is part of the fun of making your own pizzas. Carolyn crimps the edge of the pizza dough,* **above,** *before putting on the filling.*

HERBS OF NECESSITY

I n his columns in the *New York Times* and in his cookbooks, Craig Claiborne has been instrumental in educating Americans about good food and good eating. He's given us the confidence to approach the classic dishes of *haute cuisine*, introduced us to the simple fare of French *cafés* and Italian *trattorias*, and made us recognize the treasures of our own regional cooking.

Mr. Claiborne's current mission is to teach us that fine food doesn't have to mean rich sauces and high fat content; that we can eat well and stay healthy at the same time. "People who damn *nouvelle cuisine* are imprisoned by their own thinking," he says. "But the professional kitchen invariably influences the private kitchen, so they will have to learn to break out of tradition."

When his health recently forced him to go on a low-salt diet, Mr. Claiborne developed a way of cooking that leaves in the taste while taking out most of the salt and much of the fat—just the kind of food most people want these days. To eliminate salt from the diet, he substitutes herbs and spices. Although not an avid gardener (in fact, he's landscaped his yard with natural grasses and shrubs to minimize upkeep), he does have a small herb garden outside his kitchen door where he grows the herbs he uses most: tarragon, parsley, rosemary, basil, sage, and thyme. He grows mint outdoors, too, in a pot to contain the roots.

Midweek, Mr. Claiborne spends a few days in New York to check in at the *Times,* then hurries back to his secluded East Hampton house. There, he devises his recipes at a large marble work space in the skylighted, efficient kitchen he designed. Much of the kitchen equipment is of professional size and quality, like the large restaurant range, fast, powerful dishwashers, and temperature-controlled wine-storage units.

Mr. Claiborne works with an ease that comes only from experience. For the meatball dish here, he chops the garlic by hand. "Chopping it in a processor changes the taste," he claims. He always chops onions by hand, too, for texture, unless he's "expecting hordes of people"—then he breaks down and uses a processor. The blend of herbs in this dish, finished with a generous sprinkling of parsley, is so perfect that only the most addicted salt lovers will be tempted to reach for the saltshaker.

Craig Claiborne plants only those herbs he uses most in his small garden. Mint is grown in a pot to contain the spreading roots.

The ingredients for veal meatballs with tomato sauce share space with fresh potted herbs on the work island in Craig Claiborne's kitchen, **above**. To keep the meat from sticking to his hands, he flours them lightly, **below**, before starting to shape the meatballs.

The tarragon-flavored meatballs, **below**, are browned in olive oil before being simmered in the hearty tomato sauce. Perfectly cooked pasta is topped with the tender tarragon veal meatballs in zesty tomato sauce, **opposite**, before serving.

190

VEAL MEATBALLS WITH TARRAGON

Serves 4 to 6

- ¾ pound ground lean veal
- 1 tablespoon butter
- ¾ cup finely chopped onion
- 1 teaspoon finely minced garlic
- ½ cup fine fresh bread crumbs
- 2 teaspoons finely chopped fresh tarragon or 1 teaspoon dried
- ¼ cup finely chopped parsley
- ⅛ teaspoon freshly grated nutmeg
- 1 egg, lightly beaten
- ⅓ cup freshly grated Parmesan cheese
- 2 tablespoons heavy cream
  Salt to taste (if desired)
  Freshly ground pepper
- ½ cup all-purpose flour
- 2 to 4 tablespoons olive oil
  About 5 cups tomato sauce (recipe follows)
- 1 pound spaghetti, cooked to the desired degree of doneness

Place the meat in a bowl. In a small skillet, heat the butter and add the onion and garlic. Cook, stirring, until wilted. Add this to the veal.

Add the bread crumbs, tarragon, parsley, nutmeg, egg, cheese, cream, and salt and pepper to taste. Blend well. Chill to make the mixture easier to handle.

Shape the meat into 18 balls. Dredge lightly in flour, shaking off the excess.

Heat enough oil in a skillet to reach a depth of about ⅛ inch. Add the meatballs and cook, turning, until browned all over. Add the meatballs to the tomato sauce and simmer for about 30 minutes.

Serve over cooked, drained spaghetti.

TOMATO SAUCE

- 2 tablespoons olive oil
- ¾ cup finely chopped onion
- 1 tablespoon finely minced garlic
- 2½ cups canned imported tomatoes
- ¾ cup tomato paste
  Salt to taste (if desired)
  Freshly ground pepper
- 1½ cups water
- 2 tablespoons chopped fresh basil or 1 tablespoon dried
- ½ cup finely chopped parsley
- 1 bay leaf
- ½ teaspoon dried thyme

Heat the oil in a large saucepan or casserole and add the onion and garlic. Cook, stirring, until wilted.

Stir in the tomatoes, tomato paste, salt and pepper to taste, and 1½ cups water. Add the basil, parsley, bay leaf, and thyme. Bring to a boil, reduce the heat to low, and let simmer for 30 minutes.

NEW SALSA FROM NEW MEXICO

The cuisine of the Southwest evokes thoughts of chilis and other Mexican-inspired specialties, but as in many other parts of the country, a new style of American cooking is being practiced by the chefs of Santa Fe. It's a style that relies on the freshest produce available, grown locally when possible, and is often "influenced but never tyrannized by the local cuisine," says Jim Bibo, one of the leaders of the new American cuisine, Southwestern style.

Jim and his sister Bonnie own and manage Santacafé, a restaurant they opened six years ago after moving from New York to New Mexico. Located in a 160-year-old Spanish colonial house with a center courtyard, three-foot-thick adobe walls, and dining room fireplace, Santacafé has been acclaimed by several magazines as the prettiest restaurant in New Mexico. This is a tribute to Jim, an architect, who renovated and designed the place.

The restaurant was the first in the state to offer such innovative dishes as venison with fresh juniper berry sauce and fish mousse laced with shallots, dill, parsley, and coriander. Even the local chilis gained new sophistication when Rocky Packard, the restaurant's native New Mexican chef, transformed them into fresh chili pasta or used them in sauces that bore no resemblance to the Mexican-style *salsa*.

"Herbs are critical in this cuisine of the market," Jim says. In summer he can choose from a wide variety of herbs grown by Santa Fe gardeners, but even in midwinter there's usually at the very least basil, dill, and tarragon. Jim immediately unties the bunches of herbs he buys and puts the stems in carbonated water. "It seems to keep them fresher than plain water," he says. While the leaves should be as dry as possible, he suggests covering them with a barely damp paper or cloth towel to retard wilting.

A specialty at Santacafé is pasta with a wonderfully herby sauce that changes daily. A recipe for one of the most popular versions, Pasta Nola, originated by chef Rocky Packard, follows.

Pasta Nola, **right and opposite top,** *shares the table with an herb-laced fish mousse in the firelit dining room at Santacafé.*

PASTA NOLA

Serves 8 as a main course

- ¼ cup olive oil
- 1 pound onions, julienned
- 3 pounds tomatoes, peeled, seeded, and diced
- 1½ pounds prosciutto, julienned
- 8 large garlic cloves, crushed
- 3 cups heavy cream
- 4 tablespoons chopped fresh oregano
- 4 tablespoons chopped fresh basil
- 3½ pounds fresh egg fettuccine Whole basil leaves, for garnish Freshly ground pepper

In a skillet, heat the oil and sauté the onions and tomatoes until the onion is soft and translucent. Add the prosciutto and garlic, and sauté lightly for 2–3 minutes. Add the cream and the chopped herbs. Simmer for 30 minutes.

In a large pot of salted boiling water, cook the fettuccine until just *al dente*. Drain the pasta and place it in a warmed serving bowl. Pour the sauce over the hot pasta and serve, garnished with whole basil leaves and lots of freshly ground pepper.

Snow outlines a typical Sante Fe adobe building, **center**. *Drying chili peppers hang from a porch beam,* **above**.

193

A CALIFORNIAN'S WAY WITH HERBS

I n his native California, Jonathan Waxman used his talent for innovation and the state's bountiful fresh produce to become a leader of the new American cuisine. Now he's brought his cooking style to New York, where he and wine merchant Melvyn Masters have opened Jams, a small, stylish restaurant on Manhattan's Upper East Side.

Jonathan's approach to food is a combination of the classic cooking techniques he studied at La Varenne, the *nouvelle cuisine* influences he absorbed while working in France, and the innovative cooking style he learned during a stint with Alice Waters at Chez Panisse in California.

His California background is evident in the restaurant's food and design. Every dish that comes from Jams's open stainless-steel-and-brick kitchen is cooked simply but with a sense of sophistication, using the best and freshest ingredients available. Fish and meats are grilled over mesquite or other pungent wood; preformed charcoal, says Jonathan, "adds nothing but a chemical taste." Delicate sauces are made by traditional methods, but are prepared in minutes rather than simmered for hours.

Whereas in classic French cooking, herbs are used "as background in the flavoring, or lumped together in mixes where they are indistinguishable," says Jonathan, they are an important ingredient in his own personal cuisine. He discovered the difference they could make when his mother mistakenly added lemon thyme instead of regular thyme to a dish she was preparing. "It was a mistake but it worked," he says.

To use herbs well, he advises, "you must take time and develop different tastes. At Chez Panisse, there were always four pots of herbs in the kitchen and the chefs could choose what they wanted to use. This was a remarkable way to learn, and an idea someone just beginning to cook with herbs might copy."

Like many other good cooks, Jonathan thinks that rosemary is probably the most misused herb. "You must be judicious," he cautions, "but it's incomparable when it's handled correctly. For example, lamb cooked with pine nuts, garlic, and rosemary is superb, but without the rosemary the dish somehow loses its light, ethereal quality."

In California, Jonathan could find fresh herbs of every variety almost year round. But he discovered that those being grown outside their natural season seemed out of synch in a dish with in-season ingredients. "I only make herbs that are in season an important ingredient; out-of-season herbs are relegated to background flavor."

In New York, local herb farms and a weekly shipment of herbs from California supply Jams's kitchen. Jonathan adds herbs with a deft touch to recipes like the following quick-grilled chicken breasts stuffed with basil and goat cheese.

194

Jonathan Waxman, **above,** *prepares chicken breasts at Jams. The skin must be separated from the meat,* **above right,** *before basil is slipped under it. Perfectly steamed miniature turnips and zucchini,* **opposite,** *accompany the goat cheese-stuffed chicken breast. The chicken breasts can be served at room temperature on a bed of mixed greens,* **below.**

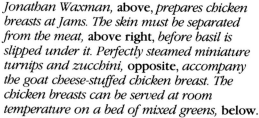

pocket and gently close the opening with your hands. Do not sew or use skewers. Put 2 basil leaves directly on the top of the chicken breast and close the skin over them. Reserve the remaining basil for garnish. Season with salt and freshly ground pepper to taste.

Grill the chicken breasts for approximately 3 to 5 minutes per side over a moderately high wood fire. (If you don't have access to a grill or hibachi, you can sauté the chicken breasts in a little olive oil over moderately high heat.)

To serve, pour one-fourth of the Basil Cream Sauce on each plate, place the chicken breast on top; garnish with julienned basil.

These chicken breasts are not only delicious but also versatile. They can be served without the sauce at room temperature as a luncheon dish. Place the chicken breasts on top of a mixture of greens (Jonathan uses a combination of *radicchio* for color, *mâche,* and endive) dressed with a light vinaigrette. Garnish the breast with a sprig of fresh basil.

CHICKEN WITH GOAT CHEESE AND BASIL

Serves 4

 2 whole chicken breasts with the first joint of the wings and skin attached, split
 3 to 4 ounces soft fresh goat cheese (domestic, if possible)
 1 small bunch of fresh basil
    Salt and freshly ground pepper
    Basil Cream Sauce (recipe follows)

Carefully bone the chicken breasts, leaving the wing joint attached. Trim the wings off at the first joint; the meaty first joint will remain attached to the breast (or have your butcher do this). Work so that you leave as much skin on the breast as possible. Gently lift this skin from the tail end of the breast back toward the wing. Carefully cut a pocket in the center of the breast on the side away from the wing. The pocket should be about 1 by 2 inches.

For each pocket, cut off a small 1-ounce piece of goat cheese and wrap 2 or 3 basil leaves around the cheese. Place the basil-wrapped cheese in the

BASIL CREAM SAUCE

 2 shallots, chopped
 1 cup heavy cream
    Basil remaining from small bunch

In a saucepan, gently cook the chopped shallots with the cream for 5 to 6 minutes, then gently reduce the sauce by two-thirds and strain.

Just before serving, julienne the basil. Stir half of the julienned basil into the sauce. Use the other half as garnish.

195

OLD BAY HERBS FOR
MARYLAND CRABS

With the Maryland Crab House Andrew Silverman brings the cooking of his native state to New York City. The specialty of the restaurant, as its name suggests, are the crabs pulled from the fertile waters of the Chesapeake. Soft-shell crabs are not new to New Yorkers, but the hard-shelled crabs so well loved in the Chesapeake area and along the Gulf Coast are. From early spring through late fall, while they are in season, crabs are the most popular dish on the menu.

Only the big male crabs are used for steaming. For years they've been cooked the same way: steamed over beer and seasoned with a tantalizing mixture of herbs and spices that is the secret of their fiery flavor. In Maryland the seasoning generally used has been made by the Old Bay Company from a closely guarded fifty-year-old recipe of finely ground herbs and spices. Along the Gulf Coat a coarser-textured blend known as Crab Boil is used. (Both are available in many food stores.)

No matter how they're cooked, however, eating steamed crabs is an event. Traditionally, the crabs are heaped on a table spread with brown paper, their bright red shells covered with the spices from the steam bath. Diners are given big wooden mallets to smash open the hard shell and reach the sweet meat inside. It can be messy and at times hard work, but with a glass of icy beer to cool the palate between bites, eating spicy steamed crab is one of the most memorable dining experiences anyone can have.

MARYLAND CRAB HOUSE STEAMED CRABS

3 to 4 male Chesapeake Bay crabs per person, depending on size
Distilled white vinegar
Beer
Old Bay Seasoning or Crab Boil (from your supermarket or gourmet shop)
Chicken wire

Choose a pot large enough to hold the crabs comfortably with at least 8 inches in depth left over. Mash a piece of chicken wire to fit into the bottom of the pot, reaching about 8 inches up the sides. This will keep the crabs above the boiling liquid during cooking. Pour equal quantities of white vinegar and beer into the pot to reach 2 inches up the sides. Bring to a boil.

Dip the crabs in an ice bath for 30 seconds to stun them. (Otherwise they will claw each other when you put them in the pot and the claws may come out of the sockets.) Add the crabs to the pot; they should be about 6 inches above the liquids. Sprinkle them liberally (or to taste) with Old Bay Seasoning or Crab Boil, cover tightly, and steam for 12 to 15 minutes.

Remove the crabs from the pot and serve with a wooden board and a wooden mallet on a sturdy table covered with brown paper.

196

Succulent Chesapeake Bay hard-shelled crabs are traditionally steamed with a special blend of herbs and spices.

A GATHERING OF MUSSELS
AND HERBS

When Joy and Robert K. Lewis bought their lovely old harbor master's house overlooking Cold Spring Harbor, New York, they didn't realize they were also acquiring a handy source for fresh, succulent mussels. But one day while walking on a nearby beach, they discovered lots of glistening black mussels waiting to be scooped up by anyone with the urge to do so.

Now, when the tide is low, the Lewises frequently return to the little strip of deserted beach at the mouth of the harbor and, pails in hand, wander along the beach, gathering mussels left behind by the receding water. For weekend guests who often come along to help, the harvesting is a pleasant adventure.

So is cleaning the mussels. Everyone gathers in the garden to relax with a cool drink while Bob shows the guests his easy cleaning method. Holding the closed mussel under a running hose, he pulls off the beard (a little hairy protuberance), then, using a mussel shell as a scraper, quickly removes any dirt or barnacles from the outside. The mussel is then dropped into a pail of cold water where it stays until dinnertime to soak out any sand that remains. Soon the eager apprentices are taking turns, talking and laughing while they clean. "When everyone helps it's really more fun than work," says Joy.

The Lewises' favorite way of cooking these fresh mussels is as simple as it is delicious: they're gently steamed with a little

198

*Joy and Bob Lewis gather pails of mussels along the edges of Long Island Sound. The mussels, topped with fresh herbs from the garden, are steamed in a pot from the Lewises' collection of old enamelware, **above left.***

vermouth and flavored with a bunch of fresh herbs from the garden. Served with a platter of basil-sprinkled tomatoes and a loaf of peasant bread, then followed with a crisp green salad and some good cheese, mussels are a perfect summer meal. If there should happen to be any left over, they are removed from their shells and used the next day for a garden-and-sea salad with shrimp, crab meat, the tiniest shell pasta, peas, julienne of raw carrot, chopped shallots, a vinaigrette, and some fresh lemon thyme leaves.

STEAMED MUSSELS

Serves 4

4 pounds of mussels
1 cup dry vermouth
10 to 12 shallots, chopped
    Handful of peppercorns
    Bunch of lemon thyme or
    assorted herbs (thyme,
    tarragon, oregano, and

lemon thyme)
2 lemons, halved

Clean the mussels, removing the beard (a little hairy protuberance) and scrubbing any dirt off the shells. As you clean them, discard any that are not firmly closed. (The easiest way to check this is to grasp the shell tightly between your thumb and forefinger, then push the top shell in one direction, the bottom in the other. If the two halves of the shell slip, throw the mussel away.) Also discard any that seem unreasonably heavy; they are probably filled with sand. Once the mussels are cleaned on the outside, put them in a pail of cool water for 1 to 2 hours to soak out any remaining sand inside the shell.

When you're ready to cook, put the vermouth in a pot large enough to hold the mussels. Add the chopped shallots and peppercorns. Place the mussels in the pot and scatter the herbs on top. Cover the pot tightly and steam the mussels over high heat for 6 to 8 minutes, or until they open. Shake the pot several times during the cooking to make sure the mussels cook evenly.

Discard any mussels that have not opened. Heap the rest on a serving dish or in individual dishes. Strain the broth and pour it over the mussels. Serve with lemon halves.

*Using one mussel shell as a scraper, Bob Lewis cleans the remaining mussels under a running hose, **above**. The herb garden provides a fragrant background for dinner, **right**, and the fresh basil and nasturtiums Bob Lewis mixes with tomatoes create a centerpiece.*

On soft summer evenings the Irvines sometimes spread an antique cloth on the lawn in the shelter of some rose bushes and partake of an elegant herbal picnic with terrine of smoked trout with sorrel sauce, chicken and veal pie, a trio of salads, and delicate elderberry tarts.

COUNTRY PICNIC AT AN ENGLISH MILL

When Anna and Deryk Irvine bought Wanford Mill, their fifteenth-century house near London, it was in a sorry state of disrepair. The original timber structure had been covered with brick in the eighteenth century and remained solid, but the floors had deteriorated and the walls and ceilings were in need of restoration. An architect by profession, Deryk immediately dedicated himself to the job.

Now carefully restored and modernized, the walls painted white and old wood beams left exposed, the mill has been furnished with antique wicker and English country pieces. The large and cozy kitchen includes a country table where friends can sit and chat while Anna cooks. The millstream rushing underneath the house is a soothing backdrop for all activities.

Once the house was finished, Anna got Deryk to help her plant an herb garden. Although a few herbs are scattered among the flowers in the gardens close to the house, the main growing is done a short distance away in a row of cold frames where plants once were started. The glass covers had long since disappeared, but the remaining brick bases provided raised beds that are easy to tend. Regular and decorative bricks divide each bed into nine sections.

Because the Irvines thought the mill and its surroundings so enchanting, they wanted to share them with others, and opening the mill to bed-and-breakfast guests seemed a logical way. But bed and breakfast at the Irvines' more often than not also includes a dinner that is a testimony to Anna's talent in using herbs.

Anna and Deryk Irvine, **above,** *on the steps of their restored fifteenth-century mill.*

203

TERRINE OF SMOKED TROUT WITH SORREL

Serves 20 as an appetizer

- 1 pound fillets of Dover sole
- 1¼ pounds fillets of whiting, cod, or other firm white fish
- 1 large trout, filleted
- ½ cup milk
- 4 slices white bread
  Salt and freshly ground pepper
- 3 egg whites
- 2½ cups heavy cream
- 1 large smoked trout, filleted, cut in strips
- 20 large sorrel leaves, chopped
- ¼ cup chopped watercress plus whole leaves for garnish
- 1 package unflavored gelatin
- 2 tablespoons Cognac or brandy
  Juice of ½ lemon
  Sorrel Sauce (recipe follows)

Finely mince the sole, fish, and fresh trout. Boil the milk; remove from fire and soak the slices of bread in it. Squeeze the excess milk from the bread and mix it into the minced fish. Season with salt and pepper to taste. Set aside for 1½ hours.

Preheat the oven to 300°. Add the egg whites and cream to the fish mixture and beat well with a beater or by hand. Layer one-third of the fish mixture in a 10-inch oval terrine. Cover with a layer of half of the smoked trout; sprinkle on one-half of the chopped sorrel and watercress Continue making layers, ending with a layer of the fish mixture. Cover the dish with foil and set it in a larger pan. Add water to come halfway up the sides of the terrine. Bake for 1½ hours.

(This dish can be made the day before it is to be served or early in the day so that the terrine has time to cool before being decorated with aspic.)

Dissolve the package of gelatin in the amount of water recommended on the package. Add the brandy and lemon juice. Decorate the top of the terrine with the whole watercress leaves and pour on a thin layer of aspic. Serve with Sorrel Sauce.

SORREL SAUCE

- 2 cups plain yogurt
- 1 cup homemade mayonnaise
- 5 tablespoons chopped fresh sorrel
- 5 tablespoons chopped fresh watercress

Mix the yogurt into the mayonnaise. Stir in the chopped herbs and set aside to allow the flavors to develop.

LEMON CHICKEN PIE

Serves 10 to 12

- 2 pounds boneless chicken breasts, cut into strips
  Salt and freshly ground pepper
- 4 tablespoons chopped fresh lemon balm
- ¾ pound minced veal
- ¾ pound minced pork
- 4 slices white bread, crusts removed
  Juice and finely grated zest of 1 lemon
- 2 eggs
- 1½ pounds short pastry
- 1 egg yolk, beaten
- 2 cups aspic (optional)
  Mustard and Herb Sauce (recipe follows)

Preheat the oven to 300°. Season the strips of chicken with salt and pepper and roll them in 2 tablespoons of the chopped lemon balm. Mix the veal and pork in a large bowl.

Soak the bread in a mixture of lemon juice and water, squeeze well, and add the bread to the meat mixture, along with the remaining 2 tablespoons lemon balm, the lemon zest, eggs, and salt and pepper to taste. To check the seasoning, fry a small nugget of the mixture in a little butter or oil and taste. Adjust seasoning if necessary.

Roll out two-thirds of the pastry about ⅛-inch thick, and line the bottom and sides of a 9½-inch springform mold. Cover the bottom crust with one-third of the veal-and-pork mixture. Top with half of the chicken strips. Continue making layers, ending with the veal-and-pork mixture. Roll out the remaining pastry in a circle large enough to cover the pie. Place the pastry over the pie and trim and crimp the edges, sealing the top to the side crust. Roll out any pastry scraps and cut out leaf shapes for decoration.

Brush the crust with the beaten egg yolk and decorate with pastry leaves. They will stick to the egg glaze. Brush the leaves lightly with the yolk. Cut a tiny hole in the center of the crust with a knife and insert a metal funnel to keep the juices from running over.

Bake for 1¾ to 2 hours. The meat in the pie is done when the juices run clear. To check the juices, press on the top so they rise in the funnel. If the pastry browns before the pie is done, cover with foil for the remaining cooking time. Remove the pie from oven and cool on a rack.

The pie may be eaten as is. If you would like to add aspic, wait until the pie is cool, and pour the

The seeds from yellow-flowered mustard plants lend their sharp flavor to the sauce for Anna Irvine's Lemon Chicken Pie.

aspic through the funnel. Serve at room temperature with Mustard and Herb Sauce.

MUSTARD AND HERB SAUCE

Makes about 1¼ cups

- 2 egg yolks
- 1 tablespoon grainy mustard
  Salt and freshly ground pepper
- 2 tablespoons chopped mixed herbs (chives, tarragon, parsley, dill)
- 1 cup olive oil
  Juice of 1 lemon

Place egg yolks, mustard, salt and pepper, and herbs in the bowl of a food processor or a blender. Process for a few seconds.

Add the oil, drop by drop, with processor on, or with blender set on low. Continue adding the oil until the sauce is thick. Blend in the lemon juice. If the sauce is too thick, add 1 to 2 tablespoons boiling water.

GRILLING WITH HERBS

What could be more inviting, especially on warm summer days, than simple fresh foods, judiciously seasoned with herbs from the garden and grilled to perfection? Our cave-dwelling ancestors cooked over an open fire out of necessity, but in the years since, people all around the world have retained this simple method, which contributes a special flavor of its own. Every country has developed grilled specialties: tiny sardines in Portugal; spicy lamb kabobs in Morocco; juicy hot dogs and hamburgers in the United States.

Herbs add their own special freshness to grilled poultry, meat, fish, vegetables, and even fruits. Use them in marinades or sprinkled directly on the food; or add a more subtle herb flavor by throwing a bunch of fresh or dried herbs in the fire. Try sage for pork, fennel for fish, rosemary for chicken and lamb.

An herb basting brush is another way to add the taste of herbs to grilled foods. Gather some thyme, rosemary, hyssop, or savory and tie the sprigs together at one end, then use the bunch to baste the food with oil, butter, or a marinade as it cooks. For one last burst of flavor, toss the brush into the fire just before you remove the food from the grill.

These recipes should suggest a few new ways to use herbs on your grill and lead you into experimenting with others.

PEPPERS IN BASIL OIL

Serves 6

These grilled peppers, tossed in oil redolent of basil and garlic, are delicious as a starter or served along with simple grilled meats or chicken.

  3 garlic cloves
     Juice of 2 lemons
  1 big bunch fresh basil, finely
     chopped
     Salt and freshly ground
     pepper
  1 cup olive oil
  3 large red bell peppers

Mash the garlic in a bowl. Add the lemon juice and basil, and season with salt and pepper to taste. Pour in the olive oil and let stand for several hours. Strain if desired.

Peel the peppers: the easiest way is to char them over a flame or in a broiler, turning so they char evenly. Do this quickly to keep the peppers from getting soft. Place in a paper bag to steam. When cool, rub the skins off and cut the peppers in half lengthwise. Remove the seeds and cut the peppers into thick long strips.

String the pepper strips on skewers and grill lightly. Toss them in the basil-scented oil before serving, or purée the unstrained oil and dribble it over the pepper strips.

Grilled peppers redolent of basil, **above,** *are an appetizing way to start a meal and a great accompaniment to any simple roast meat or chicken.*

205

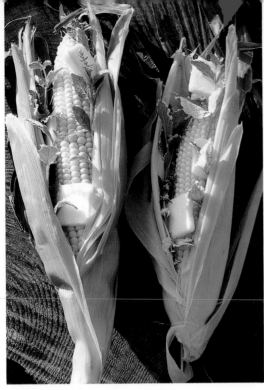

*For an interesting variation on a summer favorite, tuck a few sprigs of mint (or another flavorful herb) and some butter inside the corn husk before grilling, **above left**. Most culinary herbs can be used as a garnish. Skewered lamb, **above right**, is served on a bed of mint, one of the herbs used to flavor the marinade.*

MINTED CORN ON THE GRILL

6 ears of sweet corn in their husks
6 tablespoons butter, cut into 12 equal pieces
6 mint sprigs

Soak the corn in a pot of salt water or salted water for about 1 hour. The wet husks will steam the corn as it cooks, keeping it moist, and the salt water adds its saltiness to the corn.

Carefully peel the husks back without detaching them at the bottom and remove the corn silk. Pull the husks back up around the corn, putting 2 pieces of butter and a sprig of mint in each. Make sure the husks completely cover the kernels. Grill the corn over medium-hot charcoals, turning frequently, for 10 to 15 minutes.

206

LAMB WITH A HINT OF MOROCCO

Serves 6

An interesting combination of herbs and spices reminiscent of Morocco flavors the lamb cubes. Cooked with colorful tomatoes and zucchini and served with rice, it's a meal that's satisfying to all the senses.

2 pounds lean lamb cut from the leg into 1½-inch cubes
½ cup olive oil
1 cup dry red wine
1 small onion, finely chopped
3 tablespoons chopped fresh coriander (cilantro)
2 tablespoons chopped fresh mint
¼ cup chopped fresh parsley
2 teaspoons chopped fresh marjoram
1 teaspoon ground cumin
¼ teaspoon cayenne pepper
1 teaspoon salt

1 teaspoon Ras el Hanout (recipe follows)
18 cherry tomatoes
18 miniature zucchini or 2 large zucchini cut into 18 chunks
Yogurt Sauce (optional, recipe follows)

Place the cubed lamb in a glass or ceramic dish. Mix the remaining ingredients with the exception of the tomatoes and zucchini. Pour the mixture over the lamb, cover with plastic wrap, and let marinate in the refrigerator for 8 to 24 hours.

Drain the lamb, reserving the marinade, and string on individual skewers, allowing about 4 to 5 pieces per person and alternating it with the tomatoes and zucchini. Cook over hot coals, turning frequently, until the lamb is well done on the outside but pink inside, about 15 to 20 minutes. Baste with the reserved marinade during cooking. Serve with rice and Yogurt Sauce if desired.

RAS EL HANOUT

1 teaspoon cinnamon
½ teaspoon freshly ground black pepper
½ teaspoon freshly ground white pepper
¼ teaspoon freshly grated nutmeg
¼ teaspoon ground cloves
¼ teaspoon ground cardamom

Mix all ingredients together and store in a tightly closed jar.

YOGURT SAUCE

1 cup plain yogurt
3 tablespoons finely chopped fresh coriander (cilantro)
1 teaspoon salt

Mix ingredients together and serve at room temperature.

HERBS OF PROVENCE

The herbs of Provence grow wild on the hillsides, their intoxicating aroma a reminder of the culinary delights of the region. Provençal cuisine is pungent with thyme, rosemary, savory, fennel, marjoram, bay, and even lavender, an herb usually called upon for its scent rather than its flavor. The region's food is also enriched by garlic; freshly picked tomatoes, eggplants, peppers, and zucchini; lush melons and peaches; fish still glistening from the sea when sold in markets along the *quais;* and pale-green olive oil from the local trees.

Just as the brilliant clarity of Provence's light attracted painters like Monet, van Gogh, Renoir, Klee, Matisse, and Picasso, its wild herbs, appealing wines, and fresh produce have drawn famous cooks. Simone Beck (Simca), Roger Vergé, and Richard Olney are among those who have lived and worked here for years. Now they are being joined by younger chefs like Jean Ferrière who share their respect for the region's superb fresh ingredients.

Although cultivated herbs are available from local gardens and markets, dedicated cooks and food-lovers seek out the more flavorful wild herbs grown on the hillsides. Bundles of herbs are sold in local markets after having been gathered fresh every morning in the hills behind the Provençal coast.

To Jean Caussade, owner of St. Rémy de Provence, one of the largest suppliers of quality herbs, wild herbs gathered by pensioners and gypsies are as important as those he cultivates. "The gypsies know how to pick herbs so that the plants will grow another harvest by the time their caravan passes again," he says.

Bunches of fresh basil, tarragon, parsley, chervil, and chives tempt early-morning shoppers in the market at Grasse, **above.**

207

Fields of lavender, **left,** *dot the hillsides of Provence. The herb's rather exotic flavor is sometimes used in desserts. Tante Emilie climbs the hills behind Grasse every morning to gather wild herbs to sell in the little shop in her garage. Advice on how to use them is free.*

M. Caussade buys as much as 650 pounds of wild herbs at a time, and processes the dried leaves in the same machines his grandfather used.

Although the cooks of the region rely on the same basic ingredients, they each, like all artists, treat them in different ways. Simca's recipe for herbes de Provence, for instance, is made from four herbs from the hillsides, their dried leaves stripped from the stems, then powdered in a blender or processor and passed through a strainer before being bottled. She calls the blend MOTTS, an acromym for the recipe: one part marjoram, one part oregano, two parts thyme (her favorite herb), and one part savory. It's quite different from the coarsely textured herbes de Provence that use crumbled leaves and include lavender, rosemary, and fennel. While the coarser blend works best with grilled meats, oils, and cheeses, the more subtle powder can be added to any dish.

Two great Provençal cooks, Simca and Richard Olney, share a toast in the shade of the grape arbor on Richard's terrace.

Dried lavender, linden, and lemon verbena in a Provençal store wait to be taken home and turned into teas and potpourris.

Every time Roger Vergé goes into the Provençal countryside, he gathers wild herbs from the hillsides. These were arranged casually in a basket and used as a centerpiece at a party in his home before being taken to the kitchen of the Moulin de Mougins.

HILLSIDE HARVEST FOR MASTER CHEF

A few miles from Simca's Domaine de Bramafan lies Mougins. Once a medieval stronghold, this little hill town above Cannes has become a culinary center, with more ranked restaurants than any town in the area. Mougins was almost unknown until Roger Vergé bought the Moulin de Mougins in 1969. Within four years the restaurant, housed in an eighteenth-century mill that had been an olive oil pressing plant until the mid-1960s, was rated one of the finest in France.

Roger Vergé lived and worked in many places before he settled in Mougins, but it is in Provence that he finds it easiest to express his philosophy of cooking: "I try to be close with the natural products, to discover a harmony among the ingredients. I love Mediterranean cooking, but not the way it's done in Paris where the term Provençal means a tomato, garlic, and basil

sauce. Here we use the right herbs to bring out the flavor of each thing we cook."

M. Vergé believes, "You can add great variety to your cooking by mixing different herbs. Garlic, mint, and oregano, for instance, make a very interesting mixture," he says. He blends dry elderberry flowers with spices to season eggplant. Drawing on the cooking of North Africa, he often roasts seeds and spices before using them. "As with coffee," he says, "roasting changes the flavor entirely."

Lavender flavors some of the desserts at the Moulin de Mougins. The flowers are steeped in a brown-sugar syrup, and when the lavender sugar cools and hardens, it is ground to a powder in the food processor. The subtle lavender taste flavors puddings and other desserts.

M. Vergé makes herbs part of the food's presentation, too. Each dish is garnished with its most prominent herb in season: thyme flowers in May, for example, or basil in summer.

RACK OF LAMB WITH MILD GARLIC PURÉE

Serves 4

- 2 small racks of lamb (enough for 4)
  Thyme, salt, and pepper to taste
  A few lamb bones
- 3 tablespoons of oil
- 2 ounces shallots, chopped
- 1 sprig thyme
- 1 bay leaf
- 2 whole heads garlic, peeled
- 1 tablespoon tomato concentrate
- ½ cup wine vinegar
- 1 cup red wine
- ½ cup *crème fraîche*
- 1½ tablespoons butter

Preheat the oven to 425°. Sprinkle the rack of lamb with the thyme, salt, and pepper and roast for approximately 30 to 35 minutes or about 8 to 9 minutes per pound for medium rare.

Meanwhile, crush the bones with a cleaver and brown them in hot oil in a Dutch oven. Pour off the oil and add the chopped shallot, thyme, bay leaf, 2 cloves of the garlic, and the tomato concentrate. Cook this mixture until the shallots are transparent; then deglaze the pan with the vinegar and red wine. Add a few grains of pepper and reduce the sauce by three quarters. Then add 1 cup of water and simmer slowly to reduce by one half.

While this is cooking, put the remaining garlic cloves in a saucepan and cover with cold water. Bring to a boil and cook for a few minutes. Drain. Repeat this process five times, then put the still-warm drained garlic in the blender to make a fine purée.

Pass the first mixture through a sieve into a saucepan, add the *crème fraîche,* and cook for 2 minutes. Then bind it with the garlic purée and whisk in the butter. Put the sauce through a sieve again and taste for seasoning.

When the meat is done, let it rest for a few minutes before cutting. Cut into serving pieces and serve in a pool of the sauce, garnished with a sprig of fresh thyme.

Roger Vergé, **opposite left,** *prepares a sauce in the kitchen of the Moulin de Mougins. At the height of the season, bunches of fresh basil are puréed with fine olive oil,* **opposite right,** *then stored in the refrigerator of the Moulin to add fresh basil flavor to the menu throughout the winter. M. Vergé likes to garnish his plates,* **above,** *with herbs used in the dish. Here, a bouquet of fresh thyme accompanies a thyme-flavored rack of lamb.*

SUBTLE SEASONING OF A YOUNG CHEF

East of Mougins, in the hills above Vence, Jean Ferrière, one of Provence's new young chefs, presides over the kitchen of the Château du Domaine Saint-Martin. Built amid the medieval ruins of the Knights Templars' headquarters, this luxurious hotel overlooks the lushly verdant countryside dotted by red tile roofs and the blue of the Mediterranean in the distance. The Château has its own chickens for meat and eggs and its own fruit, vegetable, and herb gardens.

Jean learned to cook from his father, a master chef, and then perfected his skills at several two-star restaurants in France and at the Savoy in London. Now he uses his experience to adapt the classic recipes of Provence to his own style of cooking: dishes that rely on the finest, freshest produce available, local when possible, and that are not oversophisticated, not overcomplicated. "It's important to taste the flavor of the food itself," he says. "You must taste the vegetables, savor the delicate flavor of the fish. Herbs should enhance that flavor, not overcome it."

In Jean's kitchen, herbs are handled with a light touch and a spirit of invention. He uses only a bit of rosemary or thyme flowers to enhance the local lamb, already flavored by the rosemary and thyme that grow on the hills where sheep graze. He enlivens fruit salads by adding mint to a light vinaigrette of equal parts grape seed and peanut oils mixed with raspberry vinegar, salt, pepper, and a touch of cayenne. He perfumes one of his specialties, the local *loup de mer* (sea bass), with tarragon and fennel, complementing the sweet taste of the fish. The recipe for this elegant but simple dish follows.

LOUP DE MER EN PAPILLOTE

Serves 2

This sea bass typifies the refined taste and simplicity Jean seeks. As impressive as it is to serve, it's surprisingly easy to cook. The same method can be used with other fish and other herbs.

1 very fresh sea bass (about 2 to 2¼ pounds), cleaned and scaled but left whole
  Salt and freshly ground black pepper
  Fennel bulbs
6 to 8 sprigs fresh tarragon
9 tablespoons unsalted butter, cut into tablespoons
2 cups dry vermouth
1 cup heavy cream

Preheat the oven to 400°. Wash the sea bass and pat dry with paper towels. Sprinkle with salt and pepper to taste. Stuff the body cavity with a mixture of fresh chopped fennel bulb and a few sprigs of tarragon. (Reserve 3 sprigs for sauce.)

Using a sheet of parchment paper about 8 to 10 inches longer than the fish, place the fish in the center of the parchment. Take another piece of parchment and lay it over the fish. Starting on one long side, take the two edges and fold them over several times, making a tight seal. Repeat on both ends. Holding the bottom sheet of parchment on the open side up a little, pour in 1 cup of the vermouth, then seal by folding the edges together.

Place the *papillote* on a baking sheet and bake for 25 minutes. The heat of the oven will cause the *papillote* to puff up and turn golden brown.

Prepare the sauce while the fish cooks. In a medium saucepan, combine the remaining 1 cup of dry vermouth, the cream, and the reserved sprigs of fresh tarragon. Cook over high heat until the sauce is reduced almost to a glaze, about 7 to 10 minutes. Remove from the heat, remove the tarragon, and whisk in the butter, 1 tablespoon at a time.

To serve, transfer the *papillote* to a platter. Cut through the paper at the table and serve the fish. Pass the sauce separately in a sauceboat.

The simple ingredients are laid out, **opposite**, *for Jean Ferrière's delicately herbed sea bass* en papillote. *M. Ferrière,* **top**, *stuffs the sea bass with chopped fennel. A few sprigs of tarragon are tucked into the cavity,* **above**, *before the fish is enclosed in parchment paper. As the fish cooks,* **above right**, *the* papillote *holds the herb-scented steam inside.*

*By the time the fish is done, the parchment is lightly browned and puffy, **left.** To serve it, a waiter splits the browned papillote to reveal the moist, perfectly cooked fish. The Château du Domaine St. Martin is on a hilltop above Vence, **top.** An olive jar filled with geraniums, **center,** sits on the terrace. The herb garden of the Château, **above,** provides much of the produce and the herbs for M. Ferrière's specialties.*

217

FRENCH HERBS
WITH AMERICAN FLAVOR

Richard Olney, a native Iowan, became an authority on the cooking of Provence after moving to France to paint about thirty years ago. His cozy house, perched in the hills above Toulon, is surrounded by a garden filled with herbs and flowers. Farther up the hillside, a quarrylike pool has been cut out of the rock. In warm weather, a small terrace shaded by a grapevine-covered arbor serves as a dining room.

Richard's interest in cooking began when he was eight or nine years old as he watched his governess make roux. By the time he was ten, he was able to cook his father's birthday dinner. Since then, he's become a well-known cooking teacher, written two books on French cuisine, and, more recently, completed a series of cookbooks for Time-Life Books.

During his years in Toulon, Richard has grown to appreciate the honesty of the Provençal ingredients, the dishes, and the people who cook them. "The people of Provence use all the herbs that grow here," he says. "Not like in Italy where they are purists and tend to stick to oregano and sage."

As to his own herbal preference, he agrees with his good friend Simca. "If I had to choose one herb," he says, "it would be thyme. Richard also uses a lot of wild purslane in salads, gathering basketfuls of the crisp, crunchy herb from his garden. "The only two herbs one has to be careful with," he advises, "are sage and rosemary; their flavor can become too aggressive. When I grill, for instance, I just throw a little rosemary on the fire for the smoke or I use it as a brush for the marinade."

Richard Olney, **above,** *picks hyssop for grilled sardines and salads.*

Bunches of dried thyme, Richard's favorite herb, rest on the clay tile counter in the kitchen window.

*Raffia-bound bunches of dried marjoram, **opposite**, hang on the mantel beneath Richard Olney's collection of antique mortars and pestles. Richard, **right**, scatters bright-blue hyssop flowers on top of his summer salad. The salad, **left**, is garnished with peppery hyssop and nasturtium flowers and spicy basil.*

In summer, one of Richard's favorite dishes is a salad composed of what's available in the garden and kitchen. A few herbs are always used for seasoning and herb flowers are included for colorful accents as well as for their own subtle taste. The dressing is a simple vinaigrette, based on one of the herb vinegars Richard bottles and ages for at least a year. "Its flavor mellows as it ages, the same way wine's does," he says. The olive oil is from the Provençal countryside. Whether the salad is served as an appetizer or as a main course it is always accompanied by Richard's favorite local wines.

SUMMER SALAD

Serves 4

- 4 roasted red bell peppers
- 1 onion, thinly sliced
- 1 garlic clove, sliced
- 1 teaspoon coarse salt
  Freshly ground pepper
- 2 tablespoons red wine vinegar
- 6 to 8 tablespoons olive oil
  Choice of greens, including rocket, or arugula, sorrel, chicory
- 3 tomatoes, cut into bite-sized pieces
- 4 hard-cooked eggs, peeled and quartered
  Fresh herbs and herb flowers: purslane, basil, hyssop leaves and flowers, nasturtium flowers

Peel and seed the peppers, then tear them into strips and place them with their juices in a large salad bowl along with the sliced onion. (Richard Olney often uses a wide pottery bowl.)

Make a vinaigrette by mashing the garlic in a bowl with 1 teaspoon salt and a few grinds of pepper. The garlic should be completely puréed. Add the vinegar and stir well, then stir in the oil. Pour the vinaigrette over the onions and peppers and let them marinate for 2 to 3 hours.

When ready to assemble the salad, cross the salad spoon and fork over the peppers and onions. (The crossed servers keep the greens from resting in the vinaigrette and getting soggy.) Add the washed and dried greens: Arrange the tomatoes and quartered eggs on top. Then add basil leaves, the young leaves of purslane, finely chopped hyssop leaves, and scatter the blue hyssop flowers and orange nasturtium flowers on top. Toss the salad at the table before serving, making sure the ingredients are well mixed and the vinaigrette well distributed.

A buffet of herbal desserts includes ripe strawberries and orange slices, fresh coriander, and ginger; chocolate-sauced cream puffs with peppermint; frozen chocolate mousse; and a cake and frosting with lime geranium and lemon verbena.

SWEET HERBAL ENDINGS

Why not let aromatic herbs add their special touch to your desserts, too? Mint and ginger, of course, are natural dessert herbs, but roses, lavender, lemon balm, lemon verbena, and even the more aromatic bay, anise, caraway, coriander, and thyme can be used for fruits, cheese, cakes and cookies, and puddings.

Herbal "teas" are the simplest way you can add herb flavor to cakes, puddings, and sauces. Steep the herb in the liquid called for in the recipe, then cool and strain before incorporating it into the dish. Sorbets, like those on pages 226–27, use the same method. Herb sugars, made by burying a few leaves of an herb in a tightly covered jar of sugar for several weeks while the sugar absorbs the flavor, are particularly good on fresh fruits. And herb vinegars may be used on fruits and in sauces and puddings much the way you would use a liqueur.

Fresh fruits, too, can be spiced up with a few snips of herbs from the garden. Seeds or chopped herbs will add interest to baked goods for desserts—as they traditionally do in fennel-seed or poppy-seed cakes and caraway cookies.

If you give free rein to your imagination, you'll find many ways to use herbs as a sweet ending to your meal. The recipes here will serve as inspiration.

FROZEN CHOCOLATE MINT CREAM PUFFS

Makes 12 large or 24 small puffs

When mint is in abundance in the garden (or even in winter when you can substitute the dried leaves), these cream puffs filled with frozen chocolate mint mousse and covered with chocolate mint sauce are a delightfully rich but refreshing ending to a special supper. If you want a lighter dessert, serve the mousse on its own, decorated with whipped cream and sugared mint leaves.

  8 tablespoons (1 stick) butter
¼ teaspoon salt
  1 cup all-purpose flour
  4 eggs

Place 1 cup of water, the butter, and the salt in a saucepan and bring to a boil. Remove the pan from the heat and add the flour all at once. Beat with a wooden spoon until the flour has been incorporated. Return the pan to the heat and continue beating until the dough is thick and pulls away from the sides of the pan.

Preheat the oven to 425°. Remove the pan from the heat and beat in the eggs, one at a time. Drop the dough by tablespoonfuls (or teaspoonfuls for small puffs) on an ungreased baking sheet. Bake for about 30 minutes, or until golden brown. Turn the oven off and prick the cream puffs with the tip of a knife. Leave them in the oven for 10 minutes to dry out.

While the puffs are cooking, make the chocolate mint mousse filling.

223

FROZEN CHOCOLATE MINT MOUSSE

4 tablespoons chopped fresh peppermint
½ cup boiling water
2 ounces unsweetened chocolate
1 ounce bittersweet chocolate
3 egg whites
1 cup sugar
2 cups heavy cream
½ teaspoon vanilla extract

Place the mint in the boiling water and let steep for 30 minutes. Strain the mint "tea" into the top of a glass or ceramic double boiler. Add the chocolates and melt over warm water.

Beat the egg whites until they are stiff but not dry. Gradually add the sugar to the whites, beating constantly until a thick, glossy meringue forms.

Whip the cream. Gently fold the whipped cream, cooled chocolate mixture, and the vanilla into the beaten whites. Place the mixture in a pastry bag and fill the puffs. Freeze, covered, on a baking sheet until firm. Or, put in a bowl and put in the freezer until firm and serve in individual dishes.

When ready to serve, put 1 large or 3 small puffs on a plate and spoon the chocolate sauce over them. Garnish with sugared mint leaves if desired.

224

CHOCOLATE MINT SAUCE

¼ cup boiling water
2 tablespoons chopped fresh mint
9 ounces semisweet chocolate
1½ ounces unsweetened chocolate
1 tablespoon butter
½ cup milk

Pour the boiling water over the chopped mint and let steep for 20 to 30 minutes. Strain.

Melt the chocolates and butter in a double boiler over hot water. Stir in the milk and 2 tablespoons of the strained mint "tea." Continue stirring until well blended. Serve warm.

To sugar mint leaves: Wash and dry the leaves thoroughly. Brush each leaf with lightly beaten egg white and dip in superfine granulated sugar. Set on waxed paper to dry. These leaves may be stored between layers of waxed paper in a covered tin.

MARIA PRICE'S PEACH COOKIES

Makes about 4 dozen cookies

Maria Price, whose garden you saw on page 11, uses her own homemade herb jellies to turn traditional cookies into herbal delights. She often adds bits of herb to the basic recipe as well, or uses crystallized leaves from mint, lemon balm, and lemon verbena, or flowers from violets and borage or rose petals as pretty, edible decorations.

¾ cup sweet butter
½ cup milk
1 cup sugar
2 eggs
1 teaspoon baking powder
3¾ cups all-purpose flour

1 teaspoon vanilla
⅔ cup apricot jam
2 tablespoons chopped peppermint leaves
¼ cup chocolate pieces, melted and cooled
⅓ cup ground pecans
2 teaspoons rum or sherry
¼ cup water
⅓ cup red sugar
⅔ cup yellow-orange sugar
   Whole candied mint leaves, for garnish

Preheat the oven to 325°. Put the butter, milk, sugar, eggs, baking powder, and 2 cups of the flour in the bowl of an electric mixer. Blend 1 minute on low speed, scraping the bowl constantly, then beat 1 minute on medium speed while continuing to scrape the bowl. Stir in the remaining flour and vanilla. The dough will be smooth and soft.

Shape the dough into smooth ¾-inch balls (each will be half a peach). Place the cookies 1-inch apart on an ungreased baking sheet and bake on the center shelf of the oven for 15 to 20 minutes or until the cookies are brown on the bottom. Cool on a rack.

Place the tip of a small knife in the center of the flat side of each cookie and carefully rotate to make a hollow. Reserve the crumbs.

Warm the jam with the chopped mint leaves over a low flame. Mix the minted jam with 1½ cups of reserved crumbs, the chocolate, nuts, and rum. Fill the hollowed-out cookies with this mixture.

Assemble the peaches by putting the flat side of two cookies together and pressing gently. Brush each "peach" lightly with water, and immediately roll one side in red sugar for the blush. Sprinkle yellow-orange sugar on, covering the peach completely. Put a candied mint leaf in the crack at the top. Set on a rack to dry.

SPRING COMPOTE

Serves 6

This is my version of a fresh orange and strawberry compote that I had one spring in Paris. The ginger root gives it a pleasant sharpness while the coriander seems to enhance the fresh flavor of the fruits.

4 navel oranges
1 pint fresh strawberries
½ cup fruity white wine (optional)
1 tablespoon freshly grated ginger root (or to taste)
3 tablespoons chopped fresh coriander (cilantro)
   Sugar (optional)

Peel and slice the oranges over a bowl to catch the juice. Put the orange slices and the strawberries in the bowl with the juice. Add the wine if you are using it. Add the ginger and coriander, mix gently, and let stand 1 hour before serving. If the strawberries are very tart, you may want to add 1 to 2 tablespoons sugar.

LEMON 'N' LIME CAKE

Makes two 9-inch layers (1 cake)

This moist, old-fashioned cake takes on the subtle flavor of lime geranium and lemon verbena while it bakes. The same herbs scent the sugar used in the frosting, adding a subtlety to the lemon and lime juice flavoring.

CAKE

3 tablespoons finely chopped fresh lemon verbena
1 cup milk
6 to 8 lime geranium leaves
½ pound (2 sticks) butter
2 cups sugar
4 eggs, separated

3 cups all-purpose flour
2 teaspoons baking powder
1 teaspoon vanilla extract

Put the lemon verbena in a heavy enameled saucepan with the milk and heat to the scalding point. Remove from the heat and let the lemon verbena steep in the warm milk until it is cool. You can strain the herb out of the milk before adding it to the batter or leave it in, adding flecks of green to the finished cake.

Preheat the oven to 350°. Butter two 9-inch layer cake pans and line the bottoms with circles of parchment or waxed paper. Butter the paper and place 3 to 4 lime geranium leaves in the bottom of each pan.

Cream the butter. Gradually mix the sugar and continue beating until light and fluffy. Add the egg yolks, one at a time, beating well after each addition. Add the dry ingredients alternately with the milk.

Beat the egg whites until stiff but not dry. Fold one-third of the whites into the batter, then carefully fold in the remainder.

Pour the batter into the prepared pans and bake for 25 minutes, or until done. Remove the layers from the pans, peel off the parchment and lime geranium leaves, and cool on racks.

FROSTING

¼ cup milk
2 tablespoons chopped fresh lemon verbena
8 tablespoons (1 stick) butter
1 box lime geranium-flavored Confectioners' Sugar (recipe follows)
Juice of ½ lemon
Juice of ½ lime
A few drops of yellow or green food coloring (optional)
Sprigs of lime geranium or lemon verbena, for garnish

Heat the milk in a heavy enameled saucepan with the lemon verbena and let steep for 30 minutes. Strain.

Cream the butter. Gradually add the flavored sugar, along with the milk and lemon and lime juices. Beat well. The frosting should be light and fluffy. If necessary, add a little more milk. Beat in food coloring if desired.

Spread the frosting between the layers and over the top and sides of the cake. Garnish with lime geranium or lemon verbena, in blossom if possible.

LIME GERANIUM CONFECTIONERS' SUGAR

6 to 8 lime geranium leaves, slightly bruised and cut in half
1 box confectioners' sugar

Bury the geranium leaves in the sugar in a tightly closed tin and let stand at least overnight before using.

225

LEMON MINT SORBET

Makes 1 quart

This and the following recipe are the dessert versions of Peter Godoff's herbal sorbets

¼ cup fresh orange mint or spearmint leaves
2 cups sugar
5 cups water
1 cup sparkling water (preferably seltzer with no salt)
Juice of 4 to 5 lemons
Finely grated zest of 1 lemon

Prepare the mint syrup according to the basic directions on page 170.

Blend 3 cups of the syrup with the remaining ingredients in a bowl, and freeze in an ice-cream machine or in the freezing compartment of your refrigerator. If using the freezer, stir the sorbet to break up the ice crystals and refreeze. The more you stir and refreeze the sorbet, the smoother it will be.

Note: Peter finds the sparkling water gives a certain lightness to the sorbet.

PEAR GINGER SORBET

Makes 1 quart

¼ cup freshly grated ginger root
2 cups sugar
3 cups water
4 ripe pears (Bartlett, Bosc, or Anjou)
½ cup sweet white wine (young Sauterne or fruity Mosel)
1 teaspoon fresh lemon juice

Prepare the ginger syrup according to the basic directions on page 170.

Select pears that are very ripe. Peel and core them, then purée in a processor.

Blend 2 cups of the syrup, 2½ cups purée, and other ingredients together in a bowl and freeze in an ice-cream machine or in the freezer compartment of your refrigerator. If using the freezer, stir the sorbet to break up the ice crystals and refreeze. The more you stir and refreeze the sorbet, the smoother it will be.

FINGERPRINT COOKIES WITH LEMON VERBENA JELLY

Makes about 18 cookies

Here is another example of the way Maria Price uses herb jellies to turn ordinary cookies into herbal delights.

8 tablespoons (1 stick) butter, softened
¼ cup tightly packed light brown sugar
1 egg, separated
1¼ cups all-purpose flour
½ cup finely chopped nuts
Lemon Verbena Jelly (recipe follows)
½ cup confectioners' sugar
2½ teaspoons fresh lemon juice

Cream the butter. Gradually add the brown sugar and continue to beat until the mixture is light and fluffy. Beat in the egg yolk, then the flour. Gather the dough into a ball, wrap in waxed paper, and refrigerate for 1 hour.

Preheat the oven to 350°. Divide the chilled dough in half. On a lightly floured board, shape each half into a cylinder about 1 inch in diameter. With cylinders side by side, cut each into ¾-inch slices. With your hands, roll each slice into a ball. Lightly beat the egg white. Dip the ball of dough into the egg white and then into the chopped nuts. Roll between your palms to make sure the nuts are firmly stuck to the dough.

Place the cookies on lightly greased baking sheets. Dip an index finger in flour and make a deep indentation in the center of each cookie. Fill the indentation with Lemon Verbena Jelly and bake for 12 to 15 minutes, until golden brown. Cool on racks.

226

Mix the confectioners' sugar with lemon juice, stirring until smooth. Put a dab in the center of each cookie. When the icing is firm, store the cookies, with waxed paper between layers, in an airtight tin in a cool, dry place.

LEMON VERBENA JELLY

Makes about 2½ cups jelly

- 2 cups torn lemon verbena leaves
- 2½ cups boiling water
- ¼ cup cider vinegar
- 4½ cups sugar
- 1 to 2 drops yellow food coloring (optional)
- ½ bottle (3 ounces) liquid pectin

Put the torn lemon verbena leaves into a medium bowl. Add the boiling water, cover, and let stand for 15 minutes. Strain and measure out 2 cups of the infusion into a large, heavy saucepan.

Add the vinegar and sugar and mix well. Bring to a boil over high heat, stirring constantly. Add food coloring if desired. Stir in the pectin, bring to a full, rolling boil, and boil hard for 1 minute, stirring constantly. Pour into sterilized jars and seal.

Cooling lemon mint sorbet, **opposite,** *is served in a scooped-out lemon shell and garnished with a fresh mint leaf. To turn traditional cookies like these,* **left,** *into herbal treats, Maria Price fills them with a variety of her own homemade herb jellies.*

227

HERB TEAS

Herb teas can be tart and acidic, mild and fruity, refreshingly minty, or pungent and savory. While many people drink herb teas just for the flavor, over the years they've also been used for their therapeutic value: to soothe digestion, lift the spirits, calm the stomach, induce sleep, or ease the misery of a cold.

Because the flavor of herb teas is so delicate, you may find them bland and uninteresting at first. One way to get accustomed to the taste is to add a few sprigs of lemon verbena and a sprig of rosemary or a rose geranium leaf to a pot of regular tea. Each time you drink tea, add more herbs and less regular tea to the pot, and soon you'll come to appreciate the gentle, caffeine-free flavor.

You can brew herb teas just like ordinary tea by pouring boiling water over the herbs (1 teaspoon of dried herb or 1 tablespoon of fresh herb to 1 cup of water) and letting it steep, covered, for at least 5 minutes. Don't allow the herbs to steep more than 10 minutes: it can bring out a bitter taste. If you want a stronger flavor, add more herbs instead of oversteeping.

Because the flavor of barks and roots is hard to extract, you brew these as a decoction. Put the herb in cool water, bring to a simmer, and continue simmering gently for about 15 minutes. Always use a glass, ceramic, enamel, or porcelain kettle or pot since the alkaloids in herbs are extremely sensitive to metal.

You can make herb teas from a single herb or from a combination of several: the variations are limitless. Finding the one or two you like best is part of the pleasure. You can also add cloves, cinnamon, and dried citrus peel. Once you've discovered a blend you particularly like, make up a large batch and keep it in a tin.

In the summer, iced herb teas are refreshing, especially those made from mint, ginger, or hibiscus with its tart, lemony flavor. In the winter, sipping a cup of tea made from your own herbs while chatting with a friend or taking a break from your chores will be another reward from your garden.

California herbalist Norma Jean Lathrop mixes a little fresh mint with fresh lemon verbena to make a revitalizing iced herb tea for friends.

FORGOTTEN HARVEST ICED TEA

Makes ½ gallon

This is the "house" tea that Sandy Greig serves at her herb farm, pages 71–73. It relies on the leaf or "forgotten harvest" of the raspberry bush rather than the berry. Hibiscus adds a soft pink color to this tart and refreshing tea that's a delightful drink on a hot summer day.

1 quart boiling water
3 tablespoons raspberry leaves, dried and crushed
2 tablespoons lemon grass, dried
1 tablespoon hibiscus flowers, dried

Pour the boiling water over the herbs. Steep for 20 minutes. Strain into a ½-gallon container. Fill with cold water. Serve with ice and an herb leaf (or borage blossom) for garnish.

FRUIT AND SPICE HERB TEA

2 cups dried lemon verbena leaves
1 cup dried chamomile
1 cup dried orange mint
1 cup dried orange peel (see Note)
3 tablespoons whole cloves, crushed
1 6-inch cinnamon stick, crushed

Blend all of the ingredients together and store in a tightly covered tin. When ready to make tea, shake the tin well, then spoon 1 teaspoon of the tea into the pot for each cup of water. Pour boiling water over the tea and let steep 5 to 10 minutes.

Note: to dry orange peel, scrape the inside of the shells clean after squeezing the oranges for juice. Leave only the orange part of the peel (the zest). Cut in strips and set on a rack to dry. When brittle, break in small pieces and store in a covered jar.

*Bright-blue borage blossoms frozen in ice cubes, **left,** are a pretty touch for iced herb teas and other summer drinks.*

Fruit and spice herb tea, a heady blend of lemon verbena, chamomile, orange mint, and orange peel spiced with cinnamon and cloves, is perfect for an afternoon tea.

These miniature wreaths are made from simple sprigs of rosemary or lavender or heart-shaped bases covered in colorful potpourri

DIRECTORY OF HERB SHOPS AND GARDENS

This directory lists sources for all things herbal and herb gardens worth visiting across the United States as well as in Canada, England, and France. In visiting the shops, you'll find that many have interesting gardens in addition to their herbal wares.

We have grouped herbs for culinary, beauty, and medicinal uses under the simple heading "products." "Crafts" designates supplies for such items as wreaths and potpourris as well as the finished products, while "gifts" refers to specially packaged herb products or herb-related gift items like herbal hot pads, baskets, and cookware. The code letter (R) after a listing indicates a retail store; (R) (MO), a retail store that sells mail order; (MO), a mail-order-only operation. Check with individual stores to find out whether they also sell wholesale. Stores and gardens vary widely in their hours, and some may only be open seasonally; it is therefore wise to check by telephone before making a special trip. When visiting any of the sources listed, we suggest you ask about other shops and gardens in the area that might be worth a visit—and if you discover any new sources, we would be delighted to hear about them for a future directory.

UNITED STATES

ARKANSAS

CLEMENT HERB FARM
General Delivery
Larue, AR 72743
Plants, products. (R) (MO)

CALIFORNIA

BAY LAUREL FARM
West Garzas Road
Carmel Valley, CA 93924
(408) 659-2913
Bay wreaths, crafts, gifts. (MO)

FILOLI CENTER
Cañada Road
Woodside, CA 94062
(415) 364-2880
National Trust house with knot and rose gardens; gift shop.

GARDENER'S EDEN
P.O. Box 7307
San Francisco, CA 94120
(415) 428–9292
Plants, garden tools, gifts. (MO)

THE J. PAUL GETTY MUSEUM
17985 Pacific Coast Highway
Malibu, CA 90265
(213) 459-8402
Art Museum with formal Roman garden, kitchen garden; gifts.

HARMONY HILL HERBAL CREATIONS
10951 Dos Rios Townsite
Star Route 3, Box 200
Dos Rios, CA 95429
(707) 983-6805
Products for pets, gifts. (R) (MO)

HERB PRODUCTS CO.
11012 Magnolia Boulevard
P.O. Box 898
No. Hollywood, CA 91601
(213) 877-3104
Products. (R) (MO)

J. L. HUDSON, SEEDSMAN
P.O. Box 1058
Redwood City, CA 94064
Seeds. (MO)

HUNTINGTON BOTANICAL GARDENS
1151 Oxford Road
San Marino, CA 91108
(818) 405-2100
Library, herb and rose gardens.

NORMA JEAN LATHROP
Hummingbird Hill
18635 E. Sierra Madre
Glendora, CA 91740
(213) 334-4162
Crafts. By appointment only.

LOS ANGELES STATE & COUNTY ARBORETUM
301 N. Baldwin Avenue
Arcadia, CA 91006
(818) 447-8751
Public gardens, including herb and knot gardens; gift shop.

LOTUS BLOSSOM PRODUCTS
478 W. Hamilton, Suite 264
Campbell, CA 95008
(408) 248-4144
Products. (MO)

DODY LYNESS
7336 Berry Hill Drive
Rancho Palos Verdes, CA 90274
(213) 377-7040
Crafts, gifts.
(MO) or by appointment.

MAGIC GARDEN HERB CO.
P.O. Box 332
Fairfax, CA 94930
(415) 488-4331
Products. (MO)

NATURE'S HERB COMPANY
281 Ellis Street
San Francisco, CA 94102
(415) 474-2756
Products. (R) (MO)

JEANNE ROSE—HERBAL BODY WORKS
219 Carl Street
San Francisco, CA 94117
(415) 564-6785
Beauty products; classes, consultations. (R) (MO)

ROSES OF YESTERDAY AND TODAY
802 Brown's Valley Road
Watsonville, CA 95076
(408) 724-3537
Old-fashioned rose plants. (R) (MO)

SAGE HILL
12601 Koenigstein Road
Santa Paula, CA 93060
(805) 933-1840
Products, crafts, gifts; workshops.
(MO) or by appointment.

SASO HERB GARDENS
14625 Fruitvale Avenue
Saratoga, CA 95070
(408) 867-0307
Plants, crafts, gifts. (R)

TAYLOR'S HERB GARDEN, INC.
1535 Lone Oak Road
Vista, CA 92083
(619) 727-3485
Plants, seeds. (R) (MO)

COLORADO

DENVER BOTANIC GARDENS
1005 York Street
Denver, CO 80206
(303) 575-2547
Botanic gardens include herb garden; herbarium.

HERBAL CONCOCTIONS
P.O. Box 2052
7224 S. Clarkson
Littleton, CO 80122
(303) 795-6103
Plants, products, crafts, gifts; classes.
(R) (MO)

CONNECTICUT

BITTERSWEET HERB FARM
777 E. Main Street
Branford, CT 06405
(203) 488-1599
Plants, products, gifts, crafts. (R)

CAPRILANDS HERB FARM
Silver Street
Coventry, CT 06238
(203) 742-7244
Plants, seeds, products, crafts, gifts; lectures, with herbal lunch; display gardens. (R) (MO)

233

CATNIP ACRES FARM
Christian Street
Oxford, CT 06483
(203) 888-5649
Plants, products, crafts, gifts.
(R) (MO)

THE CONNECTICUT FARMER
P.O. Box 631
Ridgefield, CT 06877
(203) 794-1601
Vinegars, mustards. (MO)

THE FARMINGTON MUSEUM
High Street
Farmington, CT 06032
(203) 677-9222
Historic house with herb garden.

GILBERTIE'S HERB GARDENS
Sylvan Lane
Westport, CT 06880
(203) 227-4175
Plants, products, crafts, gifts. (R)

HEMLOCK HILL HERB FARM
Hemlock Hill Road
Litchfield, CT 06759
(203) 567-5031
Plants. (R) (MO)

LOGEE'S GREENHOUSES
55 North Street
Danielson, CT 06239
(203) 774-8038
Plants. (R) (MO)

THE NORTH GUILFORD HERBARY
GARDENS
2865 Long Hill Road
North Guilford, CT 06437
(203) 475-1175 (garden); (203)
453-2753 (shop)
Plants, products. (R) (MO)

THE SILO
Upland Road
New Milford, CT 06776
(203) 355-0300
Products, crafts; cooking classes. (R)
(MO)

WHITE FLOWER FARM
Route #63
Litchfield, CT 06759
(203) 567-8789
Plants. (MO) (800) 243-2853

DISTRICT OF COLUMBIA

THE HERB COTTAGE
Washington Cathedral
Mt. St. Alban, Washington, DC 20016
(202) 537-6230
Cathedral with herb gardens; plants,
products, crafts, gifts. (R) (MO
except plants)

MARSTON LUCE GALLERY
1314 Twenty-first Street NW
Washington, DC 20037
(202) 775-9460
Antique shop; small standard plants
and miniature Versailles planters.

THE NATIONAL HERB GARDEN
U.S. National Arboretum
3501 New York Avenue NE
Washington, DC 20002
(202) 399-5958
Knot garden; old rose garden; ten
specialty herb gardens.

ILLINOIS

CHICAGO BOTANIC GARDEN
P.O. Box 400
Glencoe, IL 60022
(312) 835-5440
Botanic gardens including herb
garden and gift shop. (R)

FRAGRANT FIELDS
Route 2, Box 199
Dongola, IL 62926
(618) 827-3677
Plants, seeds, products, crafts, gifts.
(R) (MO)

GREENFIELD HERB GARDEN
1135 Woodbine
Oak Park, IL 60302
(312) 848-5632
Crafts, gifts. (R) (MO)

SHADY HILL GARDENS
821 Walnut
Batavia, IL 60510
(312) 879-5665
Scented geraniums. (R) (MO)

INDIANA

HARMONY HERBS, INC.
527 E. Church Street
New Harmony, IN 47631
(812) 682-4657
Herb garden at Jacob Lentz House;
products, crafts, gifts. (R) (MO)

THE HERBAL GARDEN
Metamora, IN 47030
Seeds, products, crafts, gifts.
(R) (MO—Route 3, Box 136,
Osgood, IN 47037)

INDIANA BOTANIC GARDENS, INC.
626 177th Street
Hammond, IN 46324
(812) 931-2480
Products, gifts. (R) (MO)

IOWA

FLOWER VALLEY HERBS
Route 2, Box 22
Dixon, IA 52745
(319) 843-3400
Plants, products, crafts, gifts;
workshops. (R) (MO)

FOX RIDGE HERBS
4918 Red School Road
Central City, IA 52214
(319) 438-6687
Plants, products, crafts, gifts;
workshops. (R)

KANSAS

THE HERB PATCH
Box 110A
St. George, KS 66535
(913) 494-2540
Plants, seeds, products, crafts, gifts.
(R) (MO)

KENTUCKY

RUTLAND OF KENTUCKY
P.O. Box 182, Jail Street
Washington, KY 41096
(606) 759-7815
Plants, seeds, products, crafts, gifts;
workshops. (R) (MO)

LOUISIANA

GARRETT-DRAKE HOUSE
Box 316
St. Joseph, LA 71366
(318) 766-4229
Country inn with formal herb garden.

MIMOSA HERB CO.
1282 Perkins Road
Baton Rouge, LA 70806
(504) 381-9270
Plants, products. (R) (MO)

MAINE

BLACKROCK FARM
P.O. Box 19
Cape Porpoise, ME 04014
(207) 967-5783
Plants, crafts, gifts. (R) (MO except
plants)

HEDGEHOG HILL FARM
R.F.D. 2, Box 2010
Buckfield, ME 04220
(207) 388-2341
Seedlings, products, crafts, gifts;
workshops. (R) (MO)

JOHNNY'S SELECTED SEEDS
Box 602, Foss Hill Road
Albion, ME 04910
(207) 437-9294
Seeds, garden equipment. (R—
seasonal) (MO)

LIBERTY HERBS
Box 151
Liberty, ME 04949
(207) 589-4384
Plants, products, crafts, gifts; herb
dinners by reservation. (R) (MO)

MERRY GARDENS
P.O. Box 595
Camden, ME 04843
(207) 236-9064
Plants, products, crafts, gifts;
workshops. (R) (MO)

MONK'S HILL HERBS
Route 17
Readfield, ME
Mail: R.F.D. 2
Winthrop, ME 04364
(207) 685-4051
Plants, products, crafts, gifts. (R) (MO
except plants)

PINETREE GARDEN SEEDS
New Gloucester, ME 04260
(207) 926-3400
Seeds, books. (R) (MO)

MARYLAND

SUSAN BELSINGER
4388 Georgia Avenue
Brookeville, MD 20833
(301) 854-6442
Herb and cooking classes; catering.

BITTERSWEET HILL NURSERIES
1274 Governor's Bridge Road
Davidsonville, MD 21035
(301) 798-0231
Plants. (R)

COUNTRY CASUAL
17317 Germantown Road
Germantown, MD 20874
(301) 428-3434
English teak garden furniture.
(MO) or by appointment.

CAROLYN DILLE
312 Mt. Vernon Place
Rockville, MD 20852
(301) 279-5590
Herb and cooking classes; catering.

HAMPTON NATIONAL HISTORIC
SITE
535 Hampton Lane
Towson, MD 21204
(301) 823-7054
Historic site; gardens, include a
nineteenth-century herb garden.

HERBS UNLIMITED
Harborplace
301 Light Street
Baltimore, MD 21203
(301) 837-8303
Products. (R) (MO)

MARIA PRICE'S WILLOW OAK
FLOWER AND HERB FARM
8109 Telegraph Road
Severn, MD 21144
(301) 551-2237
Plants, products, crafts, gifts;
workshops; herbal luncheons by
appointment (R)

ST. JOHN'S HERB GARDEN, INC.
5525 Decatur Street
Bladensburg, MD 20710
(301) 262-5302
Products, crafts, gifts. (R) (MO)

SINKING SPRINGS HERB FARM
234 Blair Shore Road
Elkton, MD 21921
(301) 398-5566
Plants, products, crafts, gifts;
workshops; herbal lunches by
appointment. (R) (MO)

STILLRIDGE HERB FARM
10370 Route 99
Woodstock, MD 21163
(301) 465-8348
Plants, products, crafts, gifts; herbal
luncheons by appointment.
(R) (MO)

MASSACHUSETTS

BARTLETT'S OCEAN VIEW FARM
Box 899 Bartlett Farm Road
Nantucket, MA 02554
(617) 228-9403
Plants, fresh cut herbs. (R)

THE BEEHIVE HERBALS
4 Wyben Road
Southampton, MA 01073
(413) 562-1372
Plants, products, crafts, gifts. (R)
(MO)

BERKSHIRE GARDEN CENTER
Routes 102 and 183
Stockbridge, MA 01262
(413) 298-3926
Nursery with gardens including an
herb garden; herb plants, seeds,
products. (R)

BORCHELT HERB GARDENS
474 Carriage Shop Road
East Falmouth, MA 02536
(617) 548-4571
Plants, seeds.
(R—seasonal) (MO—seeds only)

THE CHANTICLEER
9 New Street
'Sconset
Nantucket, MA 02564
(617) 257-6231
French restaurant with herb garden.

CHICAMA VINEYARDS
Stoney Hill Road
West Tisbury, MA 02575
(617) 693-0309
Herb and fruit vinegars.
(R—seasonal) (MO)

COUNTRY HERBS
Box 357, Maple Street
Stockbridge, MA 01262
(413) 298-3054
Plants, seeds, products, crafts, gifts.
(R) (MO except plants)

COUNTRY LANDSCAPE
Box 251A, Rannapo Road
Sheffield, MA 01257
(413) 229-8018
Landscaping with hardy herbs.

YE CRAFTY OWL SHOPPE
755 Plymouth Street
Whitman, MA 02382
(617) 447-4584
Products, crafts, gifts; lectures.
(R) (MO)

CRICKET HILL HERB FARM, LTD.
Glen Street, P.O. Box 229
Rowley, MA 01969
(617) 948-2818
Plants, products, crafts, gifts;
workshops. (R)

FAIR GARDENS
27 Fair Street
Nantucket, MA 02554
(617) 228-4258
Country inn; herb garden;
workshops.

FERN HILL HERB FARM
177 Taylor Street
Pembroke, MA 02359
(617) 826-8745
Plants, products, crafts, gifts. (R)

FROM THREE LEVELS
164 Woburn Street
Lexington, MA 02173
(617) 862-8453
Products, gifts. By appointment.

HANCOCK SHAKER VILLAGE
P.O. Box 898
Pittsfield, MA 01202
(413) 442-8381
Shaker museum; herb garden,
products, books, crafts, gifts. (R)
(MO)

HARTMAN'S HERB FARM
Old Dana Road
Barre, MA 01005
(617) 355-2015
Plants, products, crafts, gifts. (R)
(MO)

THE HERBARY AND POTPOURRI
SHOP
P.O. Box 543
Child's Homestead Road
Orleans, MA 02332
(617) 255-4422
Plants, products, crafts, gifts.
(R) (MO)

THE HERB FARM
Barnard Road
Granville, MA 01034
(413) 357-8882
Crafts, gifts.
(MO) or by appointment.

THE HERB PATCH
20 Main Street
Concord, MA 01742
(617) 369-1948
Plants, seeds, products, crafts, gifts.
(R) (MO)

HERITAGE PLANTATION OF
SANDWICH
Box 566, Grove Street
Sandwich, MA 02563
(617) 888-3300
Museum of Americana with herb
garden.

HIDDEN BROOK HERB SHOP
1067 Middle Street
No. Dighton, MA 02764
(617) 669-5194
Products, crafts, gifts. (R) (MO)

THE LITTLE FARM
818 Main Street
Norwell, MA 02061
(617) 659-7740
Crafts, gifts. (R)

THE MISSION HOUSE
(A Property of the Trustees of
Reservations)
Sergeant Street
Stockbridge, MA 01262
(413) 298-3239
Historic house; herb gardens.

NAOMI'S HERBS
Main Street
West Stockbridge, MA 01266
Mail: Box 31, So. Lee, MA 01260
(413) 232-7763
Plants, products, crafts, gifts.
(R) (MO)

NEW ENGLAND CHEESEMAKING
SUPPLY CO.
P.O. Box 85
Ashfield, MA 01330
(413) 628-3808
Cheesemaking supplies, books.
(R) (MO)

OLD STURBRIDGE VILLAGE
Sturbridge, MA 01566
(617) 347-3362
Living museum with herb gardens;
seeds, crafts, gifts. **(R) (MO)**

PENNYROYAL PLACE
72 East Main Street
Westborough, MA 01581
(617) 366-5744
Products, crafts, gifts. **(R) (MO)**

PLIMOTH PLANTATION
P.O. Box 1620
Plymouth, MA 02360
(617) 746-1622
Living museum with herb gardens.
Seasonal.

AL SANDERS
453 Bedford Road
Carlisle, MA 01741
Drying racks. **(MO)**

SEVEN ARROWS HERB FARM
346 Oakhill Avenue
Attleboro, MA 02703
(617) 399-7860
Plants, products, crafts, gifts; classes.
(R)

THE VILLAGE STORE
999 Main Road
Westport, MA 02790
(617) 636-2572
Products, vinegar-making supplies.
(R) (MO)

BETSY WILLIAMS HERBS
155 Chestnut Street
Andover, MA 01810
(617) 475-2540
Plants, products, crafts, gifts;
workshops. **(R—seasonal or by
appointment) (MO)**

236

MICHIGAN

BACK PORCH ORGANIC HERB FARM
8098 West A-B Avenue
Otsego, MI 49078
(616) 694-6765
Plants, products, crafts; workshops.
(R) (MO)

CRANBOOK HOUSE AND GARDENS
380 Lone Pine Road, Box 801
Bloomfield Hills, MI 48013
(313) 645-3149
Estate gardens with formal herb
garden, kitchen herb garden.

DOW GARDENS
1018 West Main Street
Midland, MI 48640
(517) 631-2677
Seeds, products, crafts, gifts; classes.
(R)

FOX HILL FARM
Box 7, 440 W. Michigan Avenue
Parma, MI 49269
(517) 531-3179
Plants, products; annual Basil Festival
(July). **(R) (MO)**

MAY APPLE
211 N. Center Street
Hartford, MI 49057
(616) 621-6024
Products, gifts. **(R) (MO)**

RAFAL SPICE CO.
2521 Russell Street
Detroit, MI 48207
(313) 259-6373
Products. **(R) (MO)**

VALLEY HILL HERB AND PERENNIAL
FARM
Gillet Road, P.O. Box 176
Rapid City, MI 49676
(616) 331-6005
Crafts, gifts. **(R) (MO)**

WOODLAND HERB FARM
7741 N. Manitou Trail West
Northport, MI 49670
(616) 386-5081
Plants, products, crafts, gifts.
(R) (MO)

MINNESOTA

GERANIUM TREASURES
2718 Frontier Boulevard
Becker, MN 55308
(612) 261-4429
Crafts, gifts. **(R)** By appointment.

HERBAL DELIGHTS
P.O. Box 24045
Edina, MN 55410
Used and out-of-print herb books.
(MO)

MISSOURI

ABC NURSERY AND GREENHOUSE
Route 1, Box 313
Lecoma, MO 65540
(314) 435-6389
Plants, products.
(MO) or by appointment.

HERB GATHERING, INC. AND
PAULA'S POTPOURRI
5742 Kenwood
Kansas City, MO 64110
(816) 523-2653
Seeds, fresh cut herbs, crafts;
workshops. **(R) (MO)**

NEVADA

THE HERB PATCH
P.O. Box 583
Boulder City, NV 89005
Seeds, products. **(MO)**

NEW HAMPSHIRE

APPLE BUTTER HERB FARM
Old Westmoreland Road
Spofford, NH 03462
(603) 363-8902
Plants, products, crafts, gifts.
(R) (MO)

CANTERBURY SHAKER VILLAGE
Shaker Road
Canterbury, NH 03224
(603) 783-9977
Shaker museum with herb garden.

CRICKET HILL HERB FARM LTD.
R.F.D. Box 420
Brookfield, NH 03872
(603) 522-6503
Plants, seeds, products, crafts, gifts.
(MO)

THE HERB GARDEN
Haynes Road
Deerfield, NH 03037
(603) 463-8837
Plants, seeds, products, crafts, gifts.
(R) (MO)

HERBITAGE FARM
R.F.D. #2
Richmond, NH 03470
(603) 239-6231
Plants, products, crafts, gifts;
workshops. **(R) (MO** except plants.)

PICKITY PLACE
Nutting Hill Road
Mason, NH 03048
(603) 878-1151
Plants, seeds, products, crafts, gifts;
herbal luncheons by reservation.
(R) (MO except plants)

THE ROADSTEAD
Tuttonboro Corner
Route 171, R.F.D. #1
Ossipee, NH 03864
(603) 539-7311
Products. **(R) (MO)**

NEW JERSEY

COLONIAL PARK ARBORETUM
P.O. Box 5327
North Branch, NJ 08876
(201) 873- 2459
County park with rose gardens,
fragrance and sensory gardens
labeled in Braille. Seasonal.

GOAT WORKS INC.
R.D. #1 Box 57
Washington, NJ 07882
(201) 689-6899
Herbed goat cheeses. **(R) (MO)**

HERBALLY YOURS
P.O. Box 26, Changewater Road
Changewater, NJ 07831
(201) 689-6140
Products, crafts, gifts; classes.
(MO) or by appointment.

MITCHELL'S
Box 521
Holmdel, NJ 07733
Products, crafts, gifts. (MO)

THE ROSE JAR
R.D. #1, Mountain Road
Hopewell, NJ 08525
(609) 466-2816
Products, crafts, gifts. (MO)

WELL-SWEEP HERB FARM
317 Mt. Bethel Road
Port Murray, NJ 07865
(201) 852-5390
Plants, seeds, products, crafts, gifts;
display gardens. (R—seasonal or by
appointment) (MO)

NEW MEXICO

CLEAR LIGHT CEDAR COMPANY
Box 551, Church Road
Placitas, NM 87043
(505) 867-2925
Cedar products. (MO)

PLANTS OF THE SOUTHWEST
1812 Second Street
Santa Fe, NM 87501
(505) 983-1548
Plants. (R)

NEW YORK

ABIGAIL ADAMS SMITH MUSEUM
421 East 61st Street
New York, NY 10021
(212) 838-6878
Historic house with herb garden.

APHRODISIA
282 Bleecker Street
New York, NY 10014
(212) 989-6440
Products. (R) (MO)

APPLE COUNTRY ANTIQUES AND
HERBS
259 Lake Road
Ontario, NY 14519
(716) 265-1640
Plants, products, crafts, gifts.
(R—seasonal or by appointment)

ASTER PLACE HERBS
R.D. #1, Box 24B
Poland, NY 13431
(315) 845-8099
Plants, products, crafts, gifts.
(R—by appointment) (MO except
plants)

BACK OF THE BEYOND
7233 Lower East Hill Road
Colden, NY 14033
(716) 652-0427
Plants, products, crafts, gifts; classes
(R—by appointment) (MO)

BOSCOBEL RESTORATION
Route 9-D
Garrison-on-Hudson, NY 10524
(914) 265-3638
Historic federal period mansion with
herb and rose gardens. Seasonal.

BROOKLYN BOTANIC GARDEN
1000 Washington Avenue
Brooklyn, NY 11225
(718) 622-4433
Botanic garden including knot and
herb gardens, fragrance garden for
the blind, Shakespeare garden.
Plants, crafts, gifts.

CASA MONEO
210 West 14th Street
New York, NY 10011
(212) 929-1644
Spanish and Mexican herbs. (R)
(MO)

CASWELL-MASSEY CO., LTD
518 Lexington Avenue
New York, NY 10017
(212) 755-2254
or
21 Fulton Street
South Street Seaport
New York, NY 10038
(212) 608-5401
Products, gifts. (R) (MO)

CHERCHEZ
864 Lexington Avenue
New York, NY 10021
(212) 737-8215
Products, crafts, gifts. (R) (MO)

NANCY COOLEY
341 Durkee Lane
East Patchogue, NY 11772
(516) 289-2955
Wreaths, arrangements; lectures.
By appointment only.

COTTAGE HERB FARM SHOP
311 State Street
Albany, NY 12210
(518) 465-1130
Seeds, crafts, gifts. (R) (MO)

CRAILO STATE HISTORIC SITE
9½ Riverside Avenue
Rensselaer, NY 12144
(518) 463-8738
Museum of Dutch culture with Dutch
kitchen garden.

EMELIE TOLLEY'S HERB BASKET
Box 1332
Southampton, NY 11968
Products, crafts, gifts. (MO)

THE FARMERS' MUSEUM, INC.
P.O. Box 800, Lake Road
Cooperstown, NY 13326
(607) 547-2593
Living museum; medicinal herb
garden.

FLORILEGIUM
Box 157, Snedens Landing
Palisades, NY 10964
(914) 359-2926
Antique botanical prints.
(MO) or by appointment.

FROG PARK HERBS
R.D. 2, Frog Park Road
Waterville, NY 13480
(315) 841-8636
Plants, products, crafts, gifts.
(R) (MO except plants)

GATEHOUSE HERBS
98 Van Buren Street
Dolgeville, NY 13329
(315) 429-8366
Seeds, products, crafts, gifts;
workshops. (R—seasonal) (MO)

THE GREIG HERB FARM
Pitcher Lane
R.D. 3, Box 466
Red Hook, NY 12571
(914) 758-5595
Plants, products, crafts, gifts;
workshops with herbal teas; gardens.
(R—seasonal) (MO except plants)

THE HERB CUPBOARD
Box 375
Fort Plain, NY 13339
(518) 993-2363
Plants, products, crafts, gifts;
workshops. (R) (MO except plants)

HORTICULTURE HOUSE
217 East 83rd Street
New York, NY 10028
(212) 752-1559
Plants, landscaping. (R)

LEKVAR BY THE BARREL, INC.
(H. Roth & Sons, Importers)
1577 First Avenue
New York, NY 10028
(212) 734-1111
Products. (R) (MO)

MARDER'S GOOD GARDEN BOOKS
Montauk Highway
Bridgehampton, NY 11932
(516) 537-3700
Plants, garden books.

THE NATURALISTS
P.O. Box 435
Yorktown Heights, NY 10598
(914) 628-2124
Seeds, products. (MO)

NEW YORK BOTANICAL GARDENS
Southern Boulevard at 200th Street
Bronx, NY 10458
(212) 220-8700
Botanical garden with herb and rose
gardens; plants, gifts.
(R) (MO except plants)

WALTER F. NICKE
P.O. Box 667
Hudson, NY 12534
(518) 828-3415
Garden tools, supplies. (R) (MO)

OLD ORCHARD FARM STORE
Village Lane
Orient, NY 11957
(516) 323-2543
Plants, products, crafts, gifts. (R—
weekends only) (MO except plants)

OLD WESTBURY GARDENS
71 Old Westbury Road
Old Westbury, NY 11568
(516) 333-0048
Historic house and gardens,
demonstration herb garden.
Seasonal.

PAPRIKAS WEISS IMPORTER
1546 Second Avenue
New York, NY 10028
(212) 288-6117
Products. (R) (MO)

QUEENS BOTANICAL GARDENS
43-50 Main Street
Flushing, NY 11355
(718) 886-3800
Botanical gardens, herb garden;
plants, products, crafts. (R)

THE ROBIN'S NEST
R.D. 3, Garner Road
Averill Park, NY 12018
(518) 674-3974
Plants, seeds, products, crafts, gifts.
(R) (MO except plants)

ROBISON YORK STATE HERB
GARDEN AT CORNELL PLANTATIONS
One Plantations Road
Ithaca, NY 14850
(607) 256-3020
Herb garden on the Cornell campus.

ST. RÉMY
818 Lexington Avenue
New York, NY 10021
(212) 759-8240
Products, crafts, gifts. (R)

THE SHAKER MUSEUM
Old Chatham, NY 12136
(518) 794-9100
Shaker museum with herb garden.

SHUTTLE HILL HERB SHOP
243 Delaware Avenue
Delmar, NY 12054
(518) 439-6882
Plants, products, crafts, gifts. (R)

SON JARDIN
99 North Sea-Mecox Road
Southampton, NY 11968
(516) 283-1890
Plants. (R—seasonal)

STADIUM FARMS, INC.
1625 Stadium Avenue
Bronx, NY 10465
(212) 828-8610
Fresh cut herbs. (R) (MO)

SULTAN'S DELIGHT, INC.
25 Croton Avenue
Staten Island, NY 10301
(718) 720-1557
Products. (MO)

SUNFEATHER HANDCRAFTED
HERBAL SOAPS
R.D. #3
Potsdam, NY 13676
Herbal soaps. (MO)

TEA THYME HERB CUPBOARD
P.O. Box 473
East Islip, NY 11730
Products, crafts, gifts. (MO)

NORTH CAROLINA

BILTMORE HOUSE & GARDENS
One Biltmore Plaza
Asheville, NC 28803
(704) 274-1776
Historic house and walled garden,
including a small herb garden.

THE ELIZABETHAN GARDENS
Roanoke Island
P.O. Box #1150
Manteo, NC 27954
(919) 473-3234
Ten acres of gardens, including herb
and rose gardens; plants, gifts.

GRIFFIN'S
Route #7, Box 958
Greensboro, NC 27407
(919) 454-3362
Plants, crafts, gifts; workshops. (R)
(MO except plants)

HERBFLOWER STUDIO
Route #4, Box 393
Bamboo Road
Boone, NC 28607
(704) 264-7479
Plants, crafts, gifts. (R) (MO)

SANDY MUSH HERB NURSERY
Route #2, Surrett Cove Road
Leicester, NC 28748
(704) 683-2014
Plants, seeds, books. (R) (MO)

OHIO

BACKYARD HERBS "N" THINGS
4101 Canfield Road
Canfield, OH 44406
(216) 793-8326
Plants, products, crafts, gifts;
workshops.
(R—seasonal or by appointment)

BLUESTONE PERENNIALS
7211 Middle Ridge Road
Madison, OH 44057
(216) 428-1327
Plants. (MO)

CENTERVILLE HISTORICAL SOCIETY
89 W. Franklin Street
Centerville, OH 45459
(513) 433-0123
Medicinal herb garden.

COMPANION PLANTS
Route #6, Box 88
Athens, OH 45701
(614) 592-4643
Plants, seeds, fresh cut herbs. (R—by
appointment) (MO except fresh
herbs)

COX ARBORETUM
6733 Springboro Pike
Dayton, OH 45449
(513) 434-9005
Arboretum with modern herb
garden; plants, products, gifts.
(R—seasonal)

GARDEN PLACE
6780 Heisley Road
P.O. Box 388
Mentor, OH 44061
(216) 255-3705
Plants. (R—by appointment) (MO)

GLASSROOTS HERB FARM
8330 W. Pine Lake Road
Salem, OH 44460
(216) 533-6777
Plants, products, crafts, gifts. (R)

DAVID KAY GARDEN & GIFT
CATALOGUE, INC.
26055-D Emery Road
Cleveland, OH 44128
(800) 621-5199
(800) 972-5855 (In Illinois)
Garden tools and gifts. (MO)

POSIE PATCH STUDIO & GARDEN
3482 Gingham Frederick Road
Tipp City, OH 45371
(513) 698-5286
Products, crafts, gifts.
(MO) or by appointment.

SHAKER HERB FARM
11813 Oxford Road
Harrison, OH 45030
(513) 738-2939
Former Shaker settlement with
several herb gardens; plants,
products, crafts, gifts; classes. (R)

SWISHER HILL HERBS
4115 Swisher Road
Urbana, OH 43078
(513) 653-8730
Plants, products, crafts, gifts; classes.
(R)

WESTERN RESERVE HERB GARDEN
Garden Center of Greater Cleveland
11030 East Boulevard
Cleveland, OH 44106
Second largest herb garden in the
United States.

WOODSPIRITS HERB SHOP
1920 Apple Road
St. Paris, OH 43072
(513) 663-4327
Plants, products, crafts, gifts. (R)

OREGON

GOODWIN CREEK GARDENS
Box 83
Williams, OR 97544
Plants, products, crafts, gifts.
(R) (MO except plants)

THE HERBAL WAY, INC.
4974 Riverdale Road S.
Salem, OR 97302
(503) 364-3914
Plants, products, crafts, gifts;
seminars. (R) (MO except plants)

HERBS 'N' HONEY NURSERY
16085 Airlie Road
P.O. Box 124
Monmouth, OR 97361
Plants, seeds, books.
(MO) or by appointment.

NICHOLS HERB AND RARE SEEDS
1190 N. Pacific Highway
Albany, OR 97321
(503) 928-9280
Plants, seeds, products,
cheesemaking supplies. (R) (MO)

PENNSYLVANIA

ALLOWAY GARDENS AND HERB
FARM
456 Mud College Road
Littlestown, PA 17340
(717) 359-4548
Plants, products, crafts, gifts;
workshops with lunch. (R) (MO)

BARTRAM'S GARDEN
54th and Lindbergh Boulevard
Philadelphia, PA 19143
(215) 729-5281
Restoration of Quaker botanist John
Bartram's house and gardens,
including herb garden and gift shop.

THE COLLEGE OF PHYSICIANS OF
PHILADELPHIA
19 S. 22nd Street
Philadelphia, PA 19103
(215) 561-6050
Medicinal herb garden; file on herbal
medicine.

COUNTRYSIDE HERB FARM
Box 391
Conneautville, PA 16406
(814) 587-6331
Products and gifts. (MO)

DIONYSOS' BARN
Box 31
Bodines, PA 17722
(717) 995-5453
Plants, products, crafts, gifts. (R) (MO)

FORT HUNTER MANSION
5300 N. Front Street
Harrisburg, PA 17110
(717) 599-5751
Historic house with herb garden.

GINGHAM 'N' SPICE
P.O. Box 88
Gardenville, PA 18926
(215) 348-3595
Products, crafts, gifts. (MO)

THE HERB COTTAGE
Lincoln Highway East
R.D. #2, Box 130
Fayetteville, PA 17222
(717) 352-7733
Products, crafts, gifts. (R) (MO)

THE HERB SHOP
20 East Main Street
Lititz, PA 17543
(717) 626-9206
Products, crafts, gifts. (R) (MO)

THE HERB SHOP
R.D. #1, Box 297
Shippensburg, PA 17257
(717) 423-6701
Seeds, products, gifts. (R) (MO)

THE HIBBS HOUSE
Washington Crossing State Park
Box 322
Washington Crossing, PA 18977
(215) 493-8213
Restored farmhouse with herb
garden; plants, products, crafts, gifts;
demonstrations and classes. (R)

THE LITTLE FARM WORKSHOP
820 Andrews Road
Bath, PA 18014
(215) 759-5326
Herb drawings and miniature hand-
colored etchings. (R) (MO)

NATURE'S HARMONY
2240 Pinetown Road
Lewisberry, PA 17339
(717) 697-0580
Plants; workshops. (R) (MO)

OLD ECONOMY VILLAGE
14th and Church Streets
Ambridge, PA 15003
(412) 266-4500
Restoration of original Harmony
Society village; herb garden.

PENNSBURY MANOR
400 Pennsbury Memorial Road
Morrisville, PA 19067
(215) 946-0400
Colonial country estate of William
Penn, with kitchen garden. Seasonal.

PHYSIC HERB GARDEN AT GRAEME
PARK
859 County Line Road
Horsham, PA 19044
(215) 343-0965
Historic eighteenth-century
restoration including typical
medicinal herb garden of the time.

PLEASANT VALLEY HERB FARM
R.D. #1
Coopersburg, PA 18036
(212) 346-7118
Seminars, lectures. By appointment.

POTTSGROVE MANOR
West King Street
Pottstown, PA 19464
(215) 326-4014
Historic house with eighteenth-
century herb garden.

THE ROSEMARY HOUSE, INC.
120 S. Market Street
Mechanicsburg, PA 17055
(717) 697-5111
Plants, seeds, products, crafts, gifts;
workshops. (R) (MO except plants)

RHODE ISLAND

MEADOWBROOK HERB GARDEN
Route 138
Wyoming, RI 02898
(401) 539-7603
Plants, seeds, products. (R) (MO)

WOODSON POTTERY
P.O. Box 3633
Peace Dale, RI, 02883
(401) 783-5897
Ceramic garden markers. (MO)

SOUTH CAROLINA

WOODLANDERS, INC.
1128 Colleton Avenue
Aiken, SC 29801
(803) 648-7522
Plants. (MO) or by appointment.

TENNESSEE

BUTTERFLIES AND BLOSSOMS
Route 1, Box 236
Fayetteville, TN 37334
(615) 433-2294
Products, crafts, gifts. (MO)

MOUNTAIN FRESH HERBS &
SPECIALITIES
P.O. Box 80126
Chattanooga, TN 37411
(615) 894-1371
Products, crafts, gifts. (MO)

SASSAFRAS HERBS, INC.
Carriage House, Belle Meade
Mansion
110 Leake Avenue
Nashville, TN 37205
(615) 352-3541
Products, gifts. (R) (MO)

TEXAS

HILLTOP HERB FARM, INC.
P.O. Box 1734
Cleveland, TX 77327
(713) 592-5859
and

10001 Westheimer
Carillon Center, Space 1202
Houston, TX 77042
(713) 784-5524
Plants, products, crafts, gifts; herbal
restaurant by reservation. (R) (MO)

UTAH

LARSEN'S HERB SHOP
160 South State
Orem, UT 84057
(801) 225-4111
Seeds, products. (R) (MO)

VERMONT

CALICO HERBS
P.O. Box 250
Essex, VT 05451
(802) 878-3247
Products, crafts, gifts. (MO)

LE JARDIN DU GOURMET
West Danville, VT 05873
Seeds. (MO)

MEADOWSWEET HERB FARM
Shrewsbury, VT 05738
(802) 492-3566
Plants, seeds, products, crafts, gifts;
workshops. (R) (MO)

SHELBURNE MUSEUM
Route 7
Shelburne, VT 05482
(802) 985-3344
Restored village museum; medicinal
and fragrance herb gardens.

VIRGINIA

COLONIAL WILLIAMSBURG
Williamsburg, VA 23185
(804) 229-1000
Living village museum; herb gardens.

COUNTRY MANOR
P.O. Box 520
Sperryville, VA 22740
(703) 987-8761
Products, crafts, gifts. (R) (MO)

EARTHWORKS HERB GARDEN
NURSERY
923 N. Ivy Street
Arlington, VA 22201
(703) 243-2498
Plants. (R)

FAITH MOUNTAIN HERBS
Box 199, Main Street
Sperryville, VA 22740
(703) 987-8824
Plants, seeds, products, crafts, gifts;
classes. (R) (MO except plants)

MOUNT VERNON
(The Mount Vernon Ladies'
Association of the Union)
Mount Vernon, VA 22121
(703) 780-2000
Historic home of George Washington
with formal kitchen garden.

MUSKETTOE POINTE FARM
Box 7
White Stone, VA 22578
(804) 435-6359
Plants, crafts, gifts. (R)

OLDE ENGLISH GARDENS HERB
HOUSE
c/o Shoppes on Wyeth Green in
Lightfoot
Box 257, Route 60 West
Williamsburg, VA 23187
(804) 565-2579
Crafts, gifts. (R) (MO)

THE PINCHED POT
14B Lakeview Drive
Stafford, VA 22554
(703) 752-0088
Handmade stoneware herb items. (MO)

SWINGING BRIDGE POTTERY
S.R. 2, Box 351A
Madison, VA 22727
(703) 923-4244
Handmade herb pots and garden
markers. (MO)

TOM THUMB WORKSHOP
P.O. Box 10258
Alexandria, VA 22310
Products, crafts, gifts. (MO)

WASHINGTON

BACK TO EDEN GARDENS
332 East Pole Road
Lynden, WA 98264
(206) 398-2953
Plants, products. (R) (MO)

CEDARBROOK HERB FARM
986 Sequim Avenue So.
Sequim, WA 98382
(206) 683-7733
Plants, products, crafts, gifts. (R)

GULL HARBOR COUNTRY
P.O. Box 7482
Olympia, WA 98507
(206) 357-6840
Products, crafts, gifts. (R) (MO)

WISCONSIN

BOERNER BOTANICAL GARDENS
5879 S. 92nd Street
Hales Corners, WI 53130
(414) 425-1131
Botanical garden including herb
garden. Seasonal.

AUSTRALIA

THE FRAGRANT GARDEN
Portsmouth Road
Erina 2250
N.S.W. Australia
043-677546
Plants, seeds, products, crafts.
(MO except plants)

CANADA

ASHBY'S SEEDS
R.R. 2, Cameron
Ontario, Canada K0M1G0
(705) 359-1115
Plants, seeds.
(MO) or by appointment July–
September.

OTTO RICHTER & SONS, LTD.
Box 26
Goodwood, Ontario
Canada, L0C1A0
(416) 640-6677
Plants, seeds, products, gifts.
(R) (MO)

ROYAL BOTANICAL GARDENS
P.O. Box 399
Hamilton, Ontario
Canada L8N3H8
(416) 527-1158
Botanical gardens including a
demonstration herb garden, scented
garden, and medicinal garden.

SANCTUARY SEEDS
2388 West 4th Avenue
Vancouver, British Columbia
Canada V6K1P1
(604) 733-4724
Seeds, products. (R) (MO)

ENGLAND

Note: Many English gardens as
noted are only open a few days
each year in aid of the The
National Gardens Scheme. Please
contact them for precise information: 57 Lower Belgrave Street, London SW1W 0LR (01-730-0359).
Those shops that do mail-order
cannot ship plants to the United
States.

ALDERLEY GRANGE
Alderley, Gloucestershire
Fragrance and herb gardens.
Open in aid of The National Gardens
Scheme.

AMERICAN MUSEUM IN BRITAIN
Claverton Manor
Bath BA2 7BD
(0225) 60503
Historic house with herb, rose, and
dyer's gardens; plants, products,
crafts, gifts; demonstrations. Seasonal.
(R) (MO except plants)

ARNE HERBS
The Old Tavern
Compton Dundon
Somerton, Somerset TA11 6PP
(0458) 42347
Plants. (R) (MO)

BARNSLEY HOUSE
Burford Road
Circencester; Gloucestershire
Herb garden and potager; plants.
Open Wednesdays.

BOG FARM
Brabourne Lees, Kent
030-381-3101
Old roses and herbs.
Open in aid of The National Garden
Scheme.

BURDOCK
Billingshurst
West Sussex
Tearoom and restaurant with herb
garden.

CALISTRO DAIRY HERD
Hundred House
Wrecclesham
Farnam, Surrey
(0252) 72912
Herbed goat cheese. (R)

CANDLESBY HERBS
Cross Keys, Candlesby
Spilsby, Lincolnshire
075485-211
Plants, products, gifts; workshops.
(MO)

CHELSEA PHYSIC GARDEN
Royal Hospital Road
Chelsea, London SW3
(1)-352-5648
Educational herb garden.

CLOCK HOUSE
Denmans
Fontwell near Arundel
West Sussex BN18 0SU
Eastergate 024 368 2808
Herb garden and courses in garden
design with John Brookes.

CRANBORNE MANOR GARDENS
Salisbury, Dorset
Cranborne 248
Walled herb garden. Open seasonally
weekends and holidays.

CULPEPER, THE HERBALIST
21 Bruton Street
Berkley Square, London, W1
01-629-4559
Plants, products, crafts, gifts.
(R) (MO except plants)

EYHORNE MANOR
Hollingbourne, Kent
062-780-514
Herb gardens; small gift shop.
Open in aid of The National Gardens
Scheme.

THE HERB FARM
165 Chessington Road
West Ewell, Surrey
01-394-1290
Plants. (R)

THE HERB GARDEN
72 Maida Vale
City of Westminster
London W9 1PR
01-624-3598
Walled herb garden; plants, seeds,
products. By appointment.

THE HERB SHOP
Riverside Place, 2 St. James Street
Taunton, Somerset TA1 1JH
0823-54900
Plants, products, crafts. (R) (MO)

HOBSON'S BESPOKE PERFUMERY
The Oast House
Mead Lane
Farnham, Surrey GU9 7DY
0252-711820
Fragrant products. (R) (MO)

HULLBROOK HOUSE HERBS
Shamley Green,
Guilford, Kent
04-83-893666
Vinegars, oils. (R)

IDEN CROFT HERBS
Frittenden Road
Staplehurst, Kent TN12 ODH
05-80-891432
Walled garden, national Origanum
collection, scented garden for the
blind; plants, products, gifts, fresh cut
culinary herbs. (R)

LATHBURY PARK HERBS
Lathbury, Newport Pagnell
Bucks MK16 8LD
0908-610316
Plants, fresh cut culinary herbs.
(R—seasonal or by appointment)

LEEDS CASTLE
Maidstone
Kent ME17 1PL
Maidstone (0622) 65400
Historic castle with herb garden.

LINDEN PERFUMERY
7 Gordon Road (off Bailgate)
Lincoln, Lincolnshire
0522-42589
Fragrant products, crafts, gifts.
(R) (MO England only)

MARLE PLACE PLANTS
Marle Place
Brenchley
Near Tonbridge, Kent
089272-2304
Plants. (R)

MEADOW HERBS LTD.
Copthall Place
Anna Valley
Andover, Hampshire
0264-52-998
Crafts, gifts. (R) (MO)

NEAL'S YARD WHOLEFOOD
WAREHOUSE
21/23 Shorts Gardens
London WC2
01-836-5151
Products. (R)

NORFOLK LAVENDER, LTD.
Caley Mill
Heacham, King's Lynn
Norfolk, PE31 7JE
0485-70384
Lavender fields; tearoom and
lavender gift shop. (R) (MO)

THE OLD RECTORY
Burghfield, Berkshire
Herbaceous borders with herbs; sink
garden; plants.
Open in aid of The National Gardens
Scheme.

PARHAM PARK
Near Pulborough
West Sussex RH20 4HS
09-066-2866
Enclosed herb garden; rose garden.
Open in aid of The National Gardens
Scheme.

ROYAL BOTANIC GARDENS
Kew
Richmond, Surrey
(1)-940-1171
Botanic gardens including herb
garden and gift shop.

SCOTNEY CASTLE
Lamberhurst, Kent
Historic castle with small herb
garden. Open seasonally.

SELSLEY HERB FARM
Waterlane, Selsley
Stroud, Gloustershire GL5 5LW
Stroud 6682
Plants, products, crafts, gifts. (R)
(MO)

SISSINGHURST CASTLE GARDENS
Sissinghurst, Kent
580-712850
Vita Sackville-West's historic home
and gardens, including herb garden
and gift shop. Open seasonally.

SUFFOLK HERBS
Sawyers Farm
Little Cornard
Sudbury, Suffolk
0787-227-247
Plants, seeds. (R) (MO)

SUTTON MANOR HERB FARM
Sutton Scotney
Winchester, Hants
0962 760855
Plants. (R) (MO)

THORNBURY HERBS
Elm Grove, Thornbury
Bromyard, Herefordshire HR7 4NJ
Kyre 08854 204
Plants. (R)

THORNHAM HERB GARDEN
The Walled Garden
Thornham Magna
Eye, Suffolk IP23 8HA
Mellis 510
Theme gardens, national collection of
digitalis and achillea; plants,
products; classes (R) (MO)

TUDOR HOUSE MUSEUM
Bugle Street
Southampton, Hampshire
703-24216
Museum; sixteenth-century herb
garden. (R)

KENNETH TURNER FLOWERS
Savery Row
London W1X 9HA
01-499-4952
Herb and flower arrangements. (R)

WITHERSDANE GARDENS
Wye College
Ashford, Kent TN25 5AH
Wye 812401
Herb garden.

YORKSHIRE HERBS
Middleton Tyas
Richmond, North Yorkshire
Barton 032-577-686
Plants, fresh cut herbs, sleep pillows;
classes, lectures.

FRANCE

CHÂTEAU DE VILLANDRY
Villandry
37510 Joué-les-Tours
47-50-02-09
Historic château and gardens
including parterres, *potager,* and
herb garden.

DIRECTORY OF HERB PERIODICALS, PUBLISHERS, AND BOOKSELLERS

This directory will be helpful to anyone who wants to learn more about growing, cooking, or crafting with herbs. It lists information-filled newsletters, publishers who specialize in herb books, and booksellers who deal in rare, used, and new books on herbs, gardening, cooking, food, and wine.

HERBORISTERIE PROVENCALE CAUSSADE
(L'Herberie de Provence)
Boite Postale 30
13210 Saint-Rémy-de-Provence
(90) 92-12-00
Products, crafts, gifts. (**R**)

L'ECOLE DU MOULIN
Le Moulin de Mougins
06250 Mougins
(93) 75-78-24
Cooking school with Roger Vergé.

LE JARDIN PROVENÇAL
Galeries du Pont Neuf
2, rue du Pont Neuf
Paris
233-3346
Herb products and gifts. (**R**)

R. DE MONTFERRIER
La Giraudière
37510 Villandry
(47) 50-08-60
Herbed goat cheese. (**R**)

JEAN MUS
Avenue Frederic Mistral
Cabris
06530 Peymeinade
93-60-54-50
Landscape designer.

SIMCA
(Simone Beck)
Le Mas Vieux
Domaine de Bramaçon
06740 Châteauneuf-de-Grasse
93-60-10-03
Cooking school.

TANTE EMILIE
2 Montée du Château
Cabris
06530 Peymeinade
Herb products. (**R**)

AMERICAN HERB ASSOCIATION
P.O. Box 353
Rescue, CA 95672
(916) 626-5046
Quarterly newsletter focusing primarily on herbs for health.

THE BUSINESS OF HERBS
P.O. Box 559
Madison, VA 22727
(703) 948-7169
Bimonthly newsletter for herb businesses and serious hobbyists.

GERARD'S GARDEN
923 N. Ivy Street
Arlington, VA 22201
(703) 243-2498
Quarterly newsletter focusing on gardening.

THE HERBAL GAZETTE
P.O. Box 491
Mt. Kisco, NY 10549
(914) 278-6381
Bimonthly magazine on medicinal herbs.

THE HERB QUARTERLY
Box 275
Newfane, VT 05345
(802) 365-4392
Quarterly magazine on herb garden design, cooking, businesses, crafts, remedies, history and lore.

THE HERBAL REVIEW
34 Boscobel Place
London SW1, England
01-235-1530
Quarterly magazine published by the Herb Society on all aspects of herbs.

DIANE LEE MATHEWS
Box 134
Salisbury Center, NY 13454
(315) 429-3409
Resource books of herb shops and mail-order sources; herb cookbooks.

MEYERBOOKS, PUBLISHER
P.O. Box 427
Glenwood, IL 60425
(312) 757-4950
Books on herbs. (**MO**)

NORTHWIND FARM
Route 2, Box 75A
Shevlin, MN 56676
(218) 657-2478
Herb gardener's resource guide.

PINE ROW PUBLICATIONS
Box 428
Washington Crossing, PA 18977
(215) 493-4259
Quarterly herb newsletter (*Potpourri from Herbal Acres*) with an emphasis on crafting but including gardening and cooking; herb books.

SOUTHERN HERBS
P.O. Box 3722
Winter Springs, FL 32708
Quarterly newsletter concentrating on the special problems of gardening in hot climates and herb crafts.

WINE AND FOOD LIBRARY
1207 W. Madison Street
Ann Arbor, MI 48103
(313) 663-4894
Rare, used, new books on herbs, gardens, food. (**R**) (**MO**)

ELISABETH WOODBURN
Booknoll Farm
Hopewell, NJ 08525
(609) 466-0522
New, used, out-of-print, rare books on herbs, horticulture, landscape gardening. (**MO**) or by appointment.

INDEX